Policy Papers
in International Affairs

NUMBER 37

Why We Need Ideologies in American Foreign Policy

DEMOCRATIC POLITICS AND WORLD ORDER

Edward H. Alden
& Franz Schurmann

Institute of
International Studies
UNIVERSITY OF CALIFORNIA • BERKELEY

In sponsoring the Policy Papers in International Affairs series, the Institute of International Studies reasserts its commitment to a vigorous policy debate by providing a forum for innovative approaches to important policy issues. The views expressed in each paper are those of the author only, and publication in this series does not constitute endorsement by the Institute.

International Standard Book Number 0-87725-537-7

Library of Congress Catalog Card Number 89-82374

CONTENTS

ACKNOWLEDGMENTS

The research and writing of this paper was supported by a grant from the Institute of International Studies. Many helpful comments and suggestions on earlier drafts of the study were given by Nelson Polsby, Lowell Dittmer, and Thomas Firestone. We would also like to thank the many people who talked with us in various interviews and conversations in Washington, D.C. in July 1988; particular thanks to James Ridgeway for his insights and his hospitality. Paul Gilchrist was a patient and careful editor throughout, and strengthened the manuscript in many ways. Finally, we especially wish to thank Professor Carl G. Rosberg for his support, encouragement, and commitment to a broad dialogue on contemporary international issues.

E. H. A.
F. S.

INTRODUCTION

Since the Vietnam War era, the impact of democratic politics on the conduct of American foreign policy has become increasingly apparent, and to many observers, increasingly worrisome. It was growing internal political pressures which by most accounts finally forced America out of Vietnam (cf. Kissinger 1983: 302–69; Bundy 1979–80; Small 1988); policymakers and academic onlookers have struggled with the dilemma of how to appease similar pressures in the future without sacrificing the consistency and coherence of foreign policy. Ideologically charged and divisive public debates have raged in the 1980s over such issues as Central America and intervention abroad, the nuclear arms race and policy toward the Soviet Union, and South Africa and human rights issues in the Third World. These persistent controversies constitute evidence of an increasingly public style of foreign policy-making—the "open diplomacy" that Woodrow Wilson advocated, but that many contemporary observers view skeptically. As Destler, Gelb, and Lake have written: "We have become all too accustomed to giving our own partisan struggles priority over consistency or coherence in our foreign policies"; as a result the nation "has been undergoing a systemic breakdown when attempting to fashion a coherent and consistent approach to the world" (1984: 11–12).

In recent years, the United States has witnessed a frontal assault on the notion that foreign policy is best left to the president, his advisers, and the foreign policy bureaucracies. Foreign policy issues have become a battleground, in Congress and in the media-created "public sphere," for contending ideologies. The same value-laden public debates that shape domestic issues such as civil rights, abortion laws, gun control, drug abuse, and aid to family farmers have surfaced in the foreign policy arena. The "national interest," far from

1

providing a stable cornerstone directing presidential action in foreign policy, has become a subject of intense political dispute.*

Can an effective foreign policy emerge from this cauldron of ideologically charged democratic politics? Can a broadly based struggle over values, beliefs and ideologies be admitted into the making of foreign policy without jeopardizing vital interests? Traditional theories of diplomacy have always answered these questions negatively (cf. Lippmann 1955), but with the evident "democratization" of foreign policy since the Vietnam War, such questions are now at the heart of the foreign policy-making process.†

This paper will address these issues by trying to answer two basic questions. First, what is the impact of ideological politics on the formulation of American foreign policy? We develop a general framework for understanding the influence ideologies have had on American foreign policy, and then look explicitly at the impact of ideologies in three issue-areas: nuclear weapons and arms control, human rights, and intervention. Second, what is the relationship between ideological politics, foreign policy-making, and the larger, global changes evident in international relations in the late twentieth century? Two contrary trends are apparent. On the one hand, the world has become more economically and strategically interdependent.** At the same time, however, competing ideological groups and movements demanding often opposing forms of state action in such realms as environmental protection, human rights, and nuclear arms have been growing. Why are these developments seen as contradictory? Interdependence restricts state autonomy and constrains national action,

*On the concept of the national interest and its utility as a guide to policymakers, see esp. George and Keohane (1980).

†We are using the notion of "democratization" in much the same way it is used by O'Donnell and Schmitter in their studies of transitions from authoritarian rule in Latin America and southern Europe: "Democratization refers to processes whereby the rules and procedures of citizenship are either applied to political institutions previously governed by other principles . . . or extended to cover issues and institutions not previously subject to citizen participation" (1986). Democratization in our context, then, refers to the extension of citizen participation into foreign policy-making, from which it had previously been excluded.

**The literature on interdependence is enormous; two of the best treatments remain Cooper (1972) and Keohane and Nye (1977).

but ideological politics demand action, autonomy, and accountability from political decision-makers. Ideological pressures from both the left and right of the political spectrum call for the state to extend the exercise of its power; interdependence means that states must adapt to limitations on their power. Decision-makers find themselves trapped between the rock of declining capabilities and the hard place of increasing demands.

American policymakers have recently become acutely aware of this dilemma. Vietnam demonstrated the limitations of American military power; Japan and West Germany are challenging the hegemony of American economic power; fiscal and social crises in the Third World have underscored the limits of American investment and aid. And yet pressures have been growing on the American state for the transcendence of those limitations—from the ideological right come demands for greater military strength and assertiveness, and from the ideological left demands for arms control and disarmament and an active human rights policy abroad.

Can America's democratic political institutions, faced with such competing demands, possibly respond to the challenges of an interdependent world? Or has the "excess of democracy" paralyzed our ability to adapt to a new era in international relations? Decision-makers are now faced, many argue, with an unmanageable burden of conflicting political pressures on key issues and a powerful but fickle public opinion which undermines any coherent policy to advance American interests (see Crozier et al. 1975; Destler, Gelb, and Lake 1984). Adaptation to a complex and changing world is seen as jeopardized by moral and ideological demands made by partisans inside and outside government, each supported by substantial segments of an often ill-informed public.

As Paul Kennedy observes in his best-selling history of the great powers, the characteristic features of American democracy—the constitutional division of powers, the role of pressure groups, the influence of the mass media and public opinion—are frequently destructive of sound foreign policy. He writes that "a country needing to reformulate its grand strategy in the light of the larger, uncontrollable changes taking place in world affairs may not be well-served by an electoral system which seems to paralyze foreign policy decision-making (1987). Similarly, I.M. Destler argues that "Americans want two things that often prove incompatible in practice: democratic government (involving ongoing competition among a range of interests and perspectives) and effective foreign policy (which requires settling on specific goals and pursuing them consistently)" (quoted in Vogler and Waldman 1985).

The enormous rise of domestic political pressures on foreign policy—from the growing role of Congress to the explosion of ideologically motivated advocacy groups to the fluctuations of American public opinion—thus raises issues of both theoretical and practical significance. Theoretically it challenges traditional diplomatic notions of foreign policy as the instrumentally rational effort to respond to external events and safeguard certain well-defined national interests. The utility of the national interest as a policy guide becomes suspect when it is subject to domestic political disputes over values and beliefs; far from being an objective guide for policymakers, the national interest comes to be defined through ideological competition. Prescriptively it raises the question of whether an increasingly democratic, ideological politics can produce a coordinated, effective foreign policy.

On both theoretical and prescriptive levels, traditional notions of diplomacy are inadequate for addressing the contemporary relationship between democratic politics and American foreign policy. The traditional critique of foreign policy-making under democratic conditions is based on a partial and antiquated understanding of how foreign policy is formulated. This has led to certain fundamental misunderstandings about the requirements for successful policy, and to an overly pessimistic reaction to the rise of ideological pressures expressed through democratic channels. In foreign policy, as in domestic politics, we will argue that ideologies can play a creative as well as a constraining role by bringing widely held values to bear on policymaking. Ideological politics, which are frequently an expression of public discontent with prevailing policies, are a means for building political consensus around new policies. They are also central to the process of policy innovation—of bringing new issues and ideas onto the foreign policy agenda. By understanding more precisely the particular roles that public values and opinion, ideological movements, advocacy groups, and legislative bodies have come to play in the formulation of foreign policy, we can better understand both the costs and opportunities for American foreign policy in a democratic age.

Chapter 1

FOREIGN POLICY AND DOMESTIC LEGITIMACY: HISTORICAL AND THEORETICAL CONSIDERATIONS

I

The incompatibility of politics and policy—of domestic competition and conciliation with a clearly defined course of action—has long been axiomatic in the study of foreign policy. Modern realism, epitomized in the writings of Hans Morgenthau, treats foreign policy as the pursuit of clearly defined national interests based on a disciplined understanding of what it takes to advance national power, influence, and wealth.* Since Tocqueville it has been the accepted wisdom that democratic states are too erratic and irrational for the effective conduct of foreign policy, inclined "to obey impulse rather than prudence, and to abandon a mature design for the gratification of a momentary passion" (1945: 244).

Among the reasons why critics believe democracies cannot conduct foreign policies are these four (as summarized by Kenneth Waltz): first, democracies prefer "easy" policies in which the rewards are immediate and tangible; second, policy changes are "determined by internal pressures that have little to do with the state's situation in the world"; third, legislative attention to foreign policy issues is sporadic and disruptive; and fourth, popular opinion, which is frequently both uninformed and unpredictable, can override the wisdom of experienced decision-makers. So, as many argue today in the United States, "the people may aspire to influence foreign policy while being unable to do so intelligently" (1967: 12–14, 269).

---

*See Morgenthau (1948). On the concept of interests generally, see esp. Hirschman (1977). Two of the classic American attempts to elucidate the notion of the "national interest" are Beard (1934) and Osgood (1953). For an excellent recent treatment, see Kratochwil (1982).

The requirements for successful foreign policy are often not the same as those for domestic policy. Morgenthau argues that "the kind of thinking required for successful foreign policy must at times be diametrically opposed to the kind of considerations by which the masses and their representative are likely to be moved" (1951:223). Elsewhere he observes: "Where foreign policy is conducted under conditions of democratic control, the need to marshal popular emotions to the support of foreign policy cannot fail to impair the rationality of foreign policy itself" (1948: 7).

Contemporary critics have also seen in democratic politics an obstacle to the rational pursuit of national interests—an obstacle to be surmounted, bypassed, or circumvented as circumstances dictate. Democratic politics are seen as at best a necessary evil in the conduct of foreign policy, at worst as a source of irrational, adventurist, or simply unwise policies. In a world demanding complex and flexible policies combining subtle mixtures of cooperation and conflict, democratic institutions which divide power and undermine central decision-making, and public pressures which raise seemingly irreconcilable ethical and value issues, are seen as cumbersome and even dangerous constraints.

This criticism of democratic foreign policy is by no means unique to modern times. For more than two millennia observers have struggled with the Janus-faced behavior of democratic governments in a violent and unstable world. While generally lauding the internal liberty enjoyed in democracies, few have agreed with Kant that in conducting foreign policy "the republican constitution provides for perpetual peace" (1983: 113). Indeed, frequently quite the opposite has been apparent. A strong case can be made that when foreign policies become democratic, when they are shaped by the opinions and values of a large populace, they tend to become more aggressive. Thucydides (1954) shows how the same democratic values and institutions that made Athens a model for the Greek world ultimately inspired a foolish adventurism that destroyed both Athens itself and the independence of the Greek city-state system. Machiavelli (1970) shows how Roman republicanism channeled domestic political conflicts into external militarism. Similarly the age of British territorial expansion coincided with the internal extension of democracy through an increasingly inclusive electoral system (Hobsbawm 1987). And in post–World War II America, the same democratic idealism which gave birth to a global strategy designed to repair the ravages of war also created a more aggressive global imperialism culminating in a bloody and futile war in Vietnam.* Since the time of the Peloponnesian War it has been evident that the qualities which make democracies so vibrant internally—their innovativeness, aggressive public-spiritedness, and concern with moral issues—are questionable virtues in foreign policy. Moderation and stability, balance and caution—those qualities which are usually extolled in the inherently turbulent world of interstate relations—often seem antithetical to the principles which animate democracies.

Political realists, faced with the extension of democracy in the modern world, have sought solace in an eighteenth-century metaphor of international relations. The world is seen as a giant chessboard, and the players are national leaders who seek to move their pieces (armies, economic resources, organizational strength) to gain the optimum advantage. The autonomy of leaders is limited only by the strength of their resources in relation to those of other states at a given time. The basic purpose of the game is to triumph (win a war, sign a favorable treaty) and thus be placed to shape the rules for the future; at the very least, the goal is to survive and continue playing.

It is a game whose complexities occupied the best statesmen of the age, and in which they demanded nothing less than complete freedom of decision. Foreign policy in the eighteenth and much of the nineteenth centuries remained exclusively the preserve of the head of state and his closest ministers, with decisions then "sprung on a submissive, a confident, or a stupid people" (Lippmann 1922: 15). Not only would democratic processes have interfered with rapid policy adjustments, but, more importantly, strongly held popular values impinging on policy would have hampered the freedom of states to make the alliances needed to stabilize the balance of power.[†]

*On the democratic origins of American imperialism, see Schurmann (1974: esp. 30–46); on Britain and the United States, see Darby (1987).

†On the relationship between absolutism and the workings of the balance of power, see Gulick (1955: esp. 68–70).

The pursuit of interests could not be hampered by the strings of democratic politics.

It was Tocqueville who, as early as the 1840s, first recognized that the rise of modern democracies was undermining the homogeneous transnational aristocratic culture which had sustained this style of diplomacy and war.* Eighteenth-century monarchs had a common interest in limiting wars based on the fear that large-scale destruction would unleash uncontrollable social and political forces (Dyer 1985: 68). The nineteenth century was to bear out these fears as the forces unleashed by the French Revolution and the Napoleonic wars increasingly impinged on the aristocratic style of war and peace. In a modern democratic state, Tocqueville argued, it was no longer possible for foreign policies to be insulated from "the mighty force of public opinion" (1945: 285). Compelled to conscript mass armies and raise huge tax revenues to support their aims, the leaders of modern democracies were forced to engage the passions of citizens in the designs of the state. Material resources could no longer be translated into national power unless human resources could be harnessed for state purposes. This activation of society changed international politics from the interplay of small elites, defending national interests as *they* defined them, to a politics which depended fundamentally on the possibility of mass mobilization (Carlsnaes 1986). European rulers who sought to resist the nationalistic fervor of Napoleon's mass armies had to find similar ways to engage the passions of citizens in support of state goals. Alfred Fouillée captured the new reality when he exclaimed: "Patrie! Humanité! Avec ces mots-là on a entraîné des armées et des peuples" (1908). Political leaders of the nineteenth century came to recognize, as Britain's Joseph Chamberlain did, "the enormous accession of power that comes to any party which can raise a great ideal and touch the spirit of the nation" (quoted in Grainger 1986: 217).

What Tocqueville, Fouillée, Chamberlain, and others understood was that the nature of foreign policy had been fundamentally changed by the need for popular support. Henceforth foreign policy would have to face inward as well as outward, responding to the

---

*On the distinction between "homogeneous" and "heterogeneous" international systems, see Aron (1966: 100).

pressures of domestic legitimacy as well as to the exigencies of international relations. The "optimum" foreign policy would have to be one which was both effective internationally and supported domestically. When the success of any policy came to depend on the maintenance of popular backing, international politics acquired an ideological dimension which had previously been lacking.

The ideological element in foreign policy has been reinforced by other factors. The emergence of "total war" in the twentieth century demanded not only the lives of millions of soldiers, but the mobilization of the entire civilian populace onto a war footing. The willingness of civilian workers to keep producing for the war effort—even when faced with the massive bombing of cities and industrial sites—became as vital for war as the courage and skill of soldiers and the strategic leadership of generals. With the advent of nuclear weapons and the policy of deterrence, the involvement of the population in foreign policy became in effect total—the credibility of deterrence rests on the threat to risk the annihilation of entire societies. Complete populations thus became hostages, though by and large willingly, to national foreign policy.

At the level of "low politics," of economics and trade relations, the pattern has been similar. With the coming of the Industrial Revolution, the largely self-sufficient states of the the eighteenth century increasingly gave way to the economically interdependent states of the nineteenth and twentieth centuries. As Polanyi (1944) argues, the relative stability of the nineteenth-century balance of power can only be explained by noting the powerful industrial and financial interests in each nation favoring peace. Economic growth, expanding trade, and growing profits were all dependent on the avoidance of major war among the great powers. Interdependence meant that the conduct of foreign policy could no longer be insulated from the domestic political strength of a rising bourgeoisie. In the late twentieth century, we have witnessed the emergence of a tightly integrated world economy in which the success of national economic policies is intimately tied to the policies and prosperity of other nations. There are few concerns of national economic policy which have not in some way acquired an international dimension. Thus the prosperity of entire populations has become intimately linked to foreign economic policies—domestic bread-and-butter issues have become foreign policy issues.

The standard political wisdom has always been that popularly elected governments rise and fall on the issues of peace and prosperity. In an age of interdependence the domestic success of governments is therefore vitally dependent on foreign policy performance. International politics have come to shape the lives of individuals in the way national politics did with the rise of the nation-state. Foreign policy has become vitally dependent on domestic legitimacy—on convincing large segments of the population that their values and/or interests are served by that policy. Legitimation, which is largely a product of how the state responds to domestic political demands, has become an integral part of foreign policy formulation (see Trout 1975). Decision-makers must respond not only to pressures from abroad, but also to politics at home.

II

The need for policy elites to pursue domestic legitimacy in foreign policy has not been widely recognized in either the international relations or comparative politics literature.* Both have tended to assume the existence of a shared, consensual, national interest in the foreign policy realm which provides a firm foundation for policymaking. Yet, as we have argued, if core values themselves are subject to dispute, the national interest provides no firm touchstone for policymakers.

The legitimation of policy may, in ideal-typical terms, be based on two sorts of appeals—the appeal to interests or the appeal to values. The distinction between values and interests, even though they have often become synonymous in social science literature, is crucial to understanding the dynamics of ideological politics. Interests can be defined as benefits which accrue to individuals or collectivities—that is, they are claims that individuals or groups have to some particular good or service. The concept of interests, as it has been understood since the late eighteenth century, has centered primarily on economic

*Some of the noteworthy exceptions include Cerny (1980), McAdams (1985), and Anderson (1989).

advantage (see Hirschman 1977). An interest is thus some tangible good, like money, property, or physical security.* Values, in contrast, can be defined as beliefs held by individuals or collectivities about what is desirable or undesirable; they involve, in other words, some element of moral judgment. As Weber argues, values are concerned with the question of appropriateness, the "oughtness" of a particular action or set of actions; they provide the normative orientation for human behavior. If interests are defined by more or less rational calculations of advantage, values emerge from deeply held beliefs and standards related to memories of the past and goals for the future. They help to answer the question, as Wildavsky puts it, of "how we wish to live with other people and how we wish others to live with us."† Values which shape political preferences emerge from defending or opposing different ways of life.

Without engaging in what has become a complex debate in social science philosophy, we defer here to what strikes us as the ordinary usage of these terms. When a stockbroker, for instance, argues that the purchase of a certain stock is "in your interest," he is clearly implying that some personal benefit will accrue to you as a result of that purchase. When a friend, however, tells you not to purchase the stock because the company does business with South Africa, he is making an appeal to your values. He might agree that purchasing the stock would be in your interest: what he is arguing is that it betrays your values. In reality the two sorts of claims frequently overlap. An action which upholds one's values may also have tangible interest benefits—e.g., a believer in the Protestant work ethic may become wealthy as a result. On the other hand, an action which promotes particular interests may be justified in value terms—a phenomenon Marx noted in concluding (wrongly) that all values

---

*The original theorists of the social contract held what we would term an interest-based view of political legitimation. In both the Hobbesian and Lockean formulations, the individual sacrifices the absolute freedom he possesses in the state of nature in exchange for the sovereign's guarantee to defend certain interests—physical security in the case of Hobbes, security plus property in the case of Locke (see Hobbes 1968 and Locke 1980).

†Wildavsky does not explicitly make the interest/value distinction, but his work on political culture offers a valuable alternative to traditional interest-based evaluations of political behavior (1987).

camouflage underlying interests. Despite this overlap of interests and values, they are clearly based on distinct types of claims.

Politicians are well aware of the distinction between interests and values. When a politician attempts to build support for a policy, he relies either on interest-based appeals or on value-based appeals— or some combination of the two. Interest-based legitimation occurs when the state maintains support for a particular policy approach by providing individuals and groups with desired goods and services, or at least with a reasonable opportunity to acquire them.* A policy of defending American access to Middle East oil tends to be legitimated in interest terms—i.e., no one wants to return to the days of gasoline lines. Value-based legitimation, on the other hand, is based on an appeal to fundamental beliefs. America's continuing support for Israel, for instance, has not been based primarily on interests, but rather on the strong emotional ties between Israel and American Jews (and the political power of that constituency), historical guilt related to the Holocaust, and a widely shared sense among Americans that it is right that the Jewish people have a secure homeland.

Policies legitimated by interest appeals, as their defenders are the first to stress, are fundamentally conservative.† This is not to say that policies designed to defend interests are unchanging; indeed, in an economically and technologically dynamic world, these policies must change all the time. One of the central tasks of the statesman is to identify and respond to changing conditions in order best to safeguard whatever interests are at stake. The point is rather that interest-based politics operate within the "rules of the game" at any given time: they are oriented primarily to immediate benefits. They exclude any larger vision of change emanating from competing systems of values. For instance, the interests of states in the context of the nineteenth-century European state system were defined by the existing rules of that system—the balance of power (cf. Kratochwil

*The notion that legitimation is "interest-based" is central to a whole genre of neo-Marxist writings on the capitalist state (see esp. O'Connor 1973).

†Hirschman (1977) argues that the early proponents of "interests" as an alternative to "passions" in guiding human behavior saw interest-directed action as preferable both for its predictability (i.e., we can anticipate what others will do by assuming they will pursue their own interests) and its constancy (i.e., pursuit of interests will be steadfast and methodical).

1982). The classical balance of power was a system in which, theoretically, the pursuit of various divergent national interests could be rendered compatible. The pursuit of the balance of power involved adaptations in alliances and military strength designed to stabilize the system, preserve state sovereignty, and minimize conflict. Interests, in this classical conception, are the keystone of international order. Statesmen adapt their conceptions of interest to changing circumstances in order to preserve or promote national well-being without questioning fundamental values.

What interest politics lack is, first, a vision of how to alter circumstances and, second, the means to deal with radically new circumstances—for instance, those following the breakdown of the nineteenth-century state system. These shortcomings are particularly acute in the contemporary world, where the rules of the game have been repeatedly assaulted by global war, revolutions, and various economic, political, and cultural crises. Interest-based politics are adaptive but not creative. They tend to be confined to dealing with immediate problems, responding to discrete threats to specific interests. The fact that we distinguish between "long-term" and "short-term" interests implies a suspicion that they differ by more than just a time dimension. Interests can direct policy over a longer period only so long as the rules of the game remain in effect. Interest-based politics lack a future orientation, a vision of how to change and shape those rules, and of how to respond to a world in which changing rules are increasingly the norm.

Value politics, in contrast, which are based on appeals to people's beliefs and ideals rather than simply to their immediate interests, contain a stronger innovative dimension. They allow for the possibility that the values underlying policy, and thus the goals of policy, may shift fundamentally. A politics rooted in values is ideological politics. The pejorative connotations of the term *ideology* have frequently overwhelmed its immense utility, indeed indispensability, as an analytical concept. Ideologies are the framework through which values become linked with political action. They can best be defined, in Daniel Bell's terms, as the "conversion of ideas into social levers."*

---

*The literature on ideology is immense, and the scope of agreement on the concept relatively limited (cf. Mannheim 1936; Lichtheim 1967; Bell 1968; and, for an attempt at synthesis, Hamilton 1987: 18–36).

Ideological politics have a tripartite structure—values, ideas, and leadership.* Values are the essential beliefs and predispositions by which people judge actions, adopt broad goals, and orient their own lives. Ideas are particular understandings of how the world works and of how to change it—frequently they come from intellectuals with special scientific or technical knowledge or a broad grasp of social reality. Keynesian economics, atomic fission, and modernization theory are examples of ideas which have profoundly shaped our understanding of nature or society. Unlike values, ideas are time-specific, bound in particular social and historical contexts: they tell people how to realize their values in a variety of different circumstances. Political leadership can be seen in this context as the ability to link ideas with widely held values for the purpose of action. The end of leadership is the creation of policy, of a course of action which guides the behavior of organizations. The leader is one who can articulate a vision or program which commands a broad following (see Schurmann 1974: 28–29), and his role is to implement policies which are accepted as legitimate by the constituencies that support him. He becomes a vehicle for the values and aspirations of the constituencies he leads.

Ideological politics thus involve leadership to link ideas with values to create policies which direct the behavior of governmental organizations; in this fashion, as Weber recognized, values are the basis for political action. Ideological politics provide a powerful source of political innovation, and of legitimation for those innovations. It is no accident that the concept of ideology first emerged in the context of revolution—specifically the French Revolution (cf. Lichtheim 1967; Hunt 1984). Ideologies are fundamentally generative rather than adaptive. If interest politics are the politics of adaptation, ideological politics attempt to mold the world, or to preserve ways of life against external change. Ideological politics attempt to shape

---

*This tripartite structure has also been used elsewhere. We are grateful to Jason McDonald for pointing out Gabriel Almond's definition of a political culture as consisting of three elements: (1) an affective element, "values," that make political action meaningful; (2) a cognitive element, "knowledge," about the environment; and (3) an evaluative element that combines the first two to orient political activity (1956).

the rules of the game—not to be shaped by them. Ideologies make leadership possible, and leadership makes responses to new challenges possible. Foreign policy is very much a realm of ideological politics, despite the ritual invocations of the primacy of interests.

If ideologies can be manipulated by leaders attempting to build support for policies, the need for these appeals demonstrates the vulnerability of leaders. Elites would prefer to make policies behind closed doors, free from popular pressures, but elite competition forces politicians into the realm of values to secure popular support for policy goals. In the contemporary world such support is far from automatically granted. Ideologies which can be used to legitimate a particular system, regime, or policy can also be used by groups who wish to challenge that legitimacy. Thus ideological efforts at legitimating authority open the state to popular pressures. Ideological politics are an admission that the state requires popular support—or at the very least popular acquiescence—to pursue its policy goals. As Samuel Kernell writes, "The sensitivity of self-reliant politicians to public opinion is their vulnerability" (1986). Ideologies are evidence not of the unshakable strength of authority but of its weakness.

The reliance on ideologies is evidence that state leaders, generally more out of necessity than choice, have opened themselves up to popular pressures. They have chosen, or been forced, to appeal to widely held beliefs and values to build support for policy. As a result, they are susceptible to influences they cannot always control. The emergence of ideological foreign policies was evidence that foreign policy leaders could no longer exclude the people from those policies; in this sense, ideologies are inherently democratic.

The need for domestic legitimacy means that foreign policies become open to the pressures of citizen advocacy and public opinion. While decision-makers must continue to respond "rationally" to external events, their responses must be tempered by the equally rational need to maintain internal support. As Holsti and Rosenau put it: "A foreign policy that does not enjoy domestic legitimacy (which implies at least some degree of agreement on basic principles, ends, and means) is not likely to prove very effective over any extended period of time" (1984).

Chapter 2

IDEOLOGY AND AMERICAN FOREIGN POLICY

In the last two decades the central problem in American foreign policy has been less how to respond to challenges abroad than how to reconcile divisions at home. The attempt to find a new foreign policy consensus to replace the one lost during the Vietnam War has lasted so long that it has forced a reevaluation of the relationship between the people and foreign policy. If foreign policies are in important respects "value-driven," then the fundamental failure of contemporary foreign policy elites has been the failure to link publicly held values to the policymaking process—in other words, to build legitimacy. With Vietnam, policy was exposed to value-laden public demands, but in the last twenty years few means have been found for integrating these values into policy. The result has been that competing values remain unreconciled, and policy legitimacy remains tenuous.

There is little evidence of the so-called end of ideology, or the atrophying of democracy, when it comes to the formulation of American foreign policy. The influence of ideological politics on foreign policy has become more visible in recent years. Debates over American national interests and the means for preserving them have been overshadowed by debates, in Congress and the mass media, over the moral as well as geopolitical dimensions of American foreign policy. A wide range of policy questions have become highly symbolic issues on the public agenda—U.S. intervention in Central America, arms control and relations with the Soviet Union, South Africa and human rights abroad. On each of these issues, the role of ideological politics—the integration of values with particular political goals—has been a crucial variable explaining American behavior.

It is by now commonplace to observe that the war in Vietnam shattered what had seemed a durable foreign policy consensus; like most commonplaces, it is only partially true. The claims of cold war bipartisanship, for instance, ignore the deep domestic divisions that existed over how America should respond to communism abroad, and the highly partisan nature of the debates over China and the potential for "rolling back" communist advances (Schurmann 1974: 114–202). And post-Vietnam policy continues in many ways to reflect consensus on the central goal of containing the Soviet Union. What the Vietnam War contributed to was the reemergence of ideological pressures on foreign policy decision-makers. The legitimacy of U.S. foreign policy was severely damaged by the egregious failure in Southeast Asia, forcing political leaders to engage in a public process of authority-building.

This crumbling of policy legitimacy, exacerbated by Watergate and a general decline of public faith in government, was reflected in the "politicization" of foreign policy in the 1970s and 1980s. Since Vietnam, significant segments of public opinion have become ideologically polarized (Schneider 1987), and ideological pressure groups have become more effective in bringing competing values to bear on the formulation of policy (Destler et al. 1984). Not only are politicians generally more attuned to public opinion on foreign policy issues since the Vietnam demonstrations, but the policy process itself is more vulnerable to influence by organized advocacy groups. Foreign policy elites within the White House and Congress vie to mobilize public opinion in support of their particular foreign policy goals. The enhanced role of Congress in the process is particularly apparent. Changes in the structure and political makeup of Congress since Vietnam have created an institution which is more ideologically divided, more assertive on foreign policy, and more susceptible to the pressures of public opinion and advocacy groups. It has challenged the primacy of the executive branch in foreign policy and increased the impact of ideological politics on policy formulation.

For almost two decades, foreign policy issues have been a major staple of the public agenda. Disputes over values, over the purposes of American politics, are increasingly being conducted in the domain of foreign policy. The directions taken by American foreign policy in the future will depend on how the system adapts to this new reality in policymaking.

I

Ideological politics link the values of constituents with programs of political action. Leaders who seek support for policies through ideological appeals do so by invoking shared values, collective conceptions of right and wrong—not by emphasizing rational calculations of self-interest. For the conduct of American foreign policy, the clusters of values which are ideologically significant can be divided broadly into liberal and conservative, left and right.* While there has always existed, at both elite and public levels, a significant body of "pragmatic" or nonideological opinion which draws selectively on both liberal and conservative values, left and right ideologies have acquired increasing significance since Vietnam.* Post-Vietnam data have shown nearly 60 percent of the public consistently supporting the foreign policy arguments associated with one or the other of these two ideological stances (Mandelbaum and Schneider 1979). The strength of these divisions increases with proximity to the issues. Thus the so-called "attentive public," who are more likely to make their views heard on foreign affairs, tends to be more ideological than the "mass public," and the existence of highly consistent cleavages between these

*Mandelbaum and Schneider (1979), in their studies of foreign policy belief systems among mass publics, use three categories rather than two. They argue that mass opinion is split among three groups they call "liberal internationalists," "conservative internationalists," and "non-internationalists." The first two correspond to our divisions between left and right. The third is a kind of residual category, comprising the over 40 percent of the public who are either (1) isolationist, (2) nonideological, in the sense of displaying no consistent pattern of values, or (3) basically uninterested in foreign affairs. Since our concern is with foreign policy ideologies, and this residual category is not identified with any particular foreign policy stance, we have chosen to use only two divisions.

†Holsti and Rosenau (1984), in their study of *elite* foreign policy belief systems, also use a tripartite division of "cold war internationalism," "post-cold war internationalism," and "semi-isolationism." The first two correspond to our right-left dichotomy, while the third is a category of minor significance in their study. The authors demonstrate a remarkable consistency of ideological positions (which they see as defined largely in response to the Vietnam War) across a wide variety of issue areas.

two groups is particularly evident in surveys of policymakers and those in positions of influence (Holsti and Rosenau 1984).*

What does it mean to speak of "left" and "right" in American foreign policy? The ideological positions are not class-based, though there are some links between occupational status and political attitudes (Maggiotto and Wittkopf 1981). Also, despite the intuitive split between a generation raised on the "lessons of Munich" and a generation nurtured in the "lessons of Vietnam," the cleavages tend to cut across generational lines (Holsti and Rosenau 1984). Higher education appears to be correlated with higher interest in foreign policy issues, but education level is not consistently associated with left or right values. Many observers have proposed geographical divisions, with the more conservative regions of the South and Southwest balancing the liberal constituencies of the Northeast and Northwest— the so-called "Cowboy and Yankee" syndrome (Oglesby 1976; Maggiotto and Wittkopf 1981). The division between left and right, however, is not a regional, generational, or class-based division, but rather a dispute over values that cuts across interest cleavages. What divides left and right are not social characteristics but value disagreements about American foreign policy which transcend demographic correlates.

What are the values which characterize left and right ideologies? In Parsons's terminology, one could say that, with regard to international politics and foreign policy, left values have tended to be universalistic, while right values have tended to be particularistic. The left has historically thought in terms of universal notions of justice— of natural rights and the common fate of mankind. The Enlightenment heritage stressed the universality of human values rather than the values and ways of life of particular communities or nations. Even the Marxist emphasis on class conflict was predicated on the assumption that the proletariat represented the "universal class"—the class whose sufferings were those of all mankind and whose liberation would be that of all men. The right, in contrast, has historically stressed the defense of the group—of one's own family, community,

*The notion of an "attentive public" was originally advanced in Almond (1950); on the distinction between "attentive" and "mass" publics, see Rosenau (1961).

or nation (Mannheim 1953). They have emphasized the uniqueness of culture and language and the connection of a particular people with a particular territory. The defense of possessions and ways of life against encroachment from outside has been the central element of right values. Patriotism has historically been the codeword for belief in strong military and internal security forces, which have become the major symbols of conservative values.

In foreign policy, the struggle between left and right values has taken ideological form—through protests, advocacy group tactics, Congressional debates, and the news media—and has manifested itself at crucial points in America's international relations. The values have remained largely consistent over time, but their particular application has varied with different historical situations. In the public debates before and after the Spanish-American War, for instance, interventionist arguments emerged from the cluster of "left" values, while anti-imperialism was adopted as a response from the "right." The war was trumpeted as a crusade to free Cuba from Spanish tyranny, and its themes tied in with the concerns of American progressives and reformists (Dallek 1983). Humanitarian reform domestically and imperialist assertiveness abroad comprised the strange bedfellows of progressive politics. The subsequent anti-imperialist reaction, which emerged when the United States found itself faced with administering newly conquered territories as far away as the Philippines, arose mainly from the "right" cluster of values. Right isolationists feared that imperialism and foreign involvement threatened American self-determination and internal stability. The issue of American participation in the League of Nations after World War I raised similar concerns: left internationalists who believed the fate of America to be tied inextricably to the realization of a stable world order vied with right isolationists who saw involvement with the outside world as a poisonous threat to American liberty and institutions.

Whatever labels one gives to these two visions—the one universalist, the other particularist—they have comprised the major value dimensions of American foreign policy. Each of the issues which raised these value concerns was "resolved" largely by the temporary political triumph of an elite representing one or the other of the competing visions. The imperialism of the Spanish-American War produced an anti-imperialist reaction, and the moral internationalism spawned by World War I produced an isolationist counterattack. It was only with the coming of the cold war era that anything approaching a durable peacetime consensus was reached between proponents of left and right values.

Why was it possible to create a high degree of national consensus on foreign policy after World War II? This question has been the subject of much commentary (see Ambrose 1985; Schurmann 1974). Consensus in the political realm implies a fairly high level of agreement among key actors about which policies ought to be pursued. The "function" of consensus in a political system is to narrow the parameters of debate over policy issues. We would distinguish here between two types of consensus—value consensus and policy consensus. A value consensus is one in which all or most decision-makers and all or most of the public share the values on which a policy is based. State-funded education for all children is an example of a value consensus. A policy consensus, on the other hand, is one in which opponents agree on a particular policy as a workable compromise among competing values. Unemployment insurance, for example, is a policy which compromises between the competing values of unregulated free labor markets and the socialized control of industry.

Viewed in this fashion, the postwar containment consensus was primarily a policy consensus—a compromise between left and right values. Containment promised a vigilant stance toward the Soviets, and later the Chinese, thus accommodating the concerns of the right, and it promised the construction of a just and prosperous global order within the "free world," thus speaking to the liberal-left agenda. The various elements which comprised the containment policy were proffered by competing ideological currents—world order and the construction of international organizations coming from the liberal/left wing; anti-communism and vigilant national security from the right. Containment made these visions operational by integrating competing values and weaving them into an executive-led strategy for American foreign policy which was relatively insulated from the buffeting of ideological currents. The domestic legitimacy of containment meant that decision-makers were free to operate within the broad parameters of the consensus. The strength of containment domestically was its ability to accommodate opposing values within an overall policy framework.

This policy consensus was severely weakened by the failing American effort in Vietnam, which undermined both pillars of support for containment. The right wing saw the failure to win the war in Vietnam as a betrayal of the commitment to contain communism, a loss of "will" which threatened American national security (Podhoretz 1982). The revitalized left saw involvement in Vietnam as a betrayal of American claims to leadership of a new, peaceful global order. American policy in Vietnam satisfied neither element—indeed it openly threatened both of them by simultaneously deflating the prestige of the American military and rupturing the economic foundations of the postwar order. The result of the debacle was to undermine the containment consensus and to reopen the kind of fundamental struggle over national direction which had occurred immediately following World Wars I and II.

II

How have these competing visions impinged on American foreign policy-making? Ideological politics, we have argued, involve three components—values, ideas, and leadership. The values which drive foreign policy are fundamentally those of constituents, of the citizens policy is meant to serve. What is generally termed *public opinion* refers to the distribution of policy relevant values in a society: it is an expression of the broad goals people seek from foreign policy. While the ideas which play a role in foreign policy may still be generated within the political parties or the universities, they are increasingly being pushed by "advocacy groups"—traditional lobbying organizations or modern "think tanks" which serve as a link between values and political leadership. By linking public values with specific policy platforms, they give them politically relevant form. The final component of ideological politics—leadership—is increasingly contested between the executive and the Congress, and the struggle over values in foreign policy frequently takes institutional form in the battle between the president and members of Congress over the direction of foreign policy.

PUBLIC OPINION

The literature on the impacts of public opinion on policy has undergone enormous analytical fluctuations since Walter Lippmann, writing in the 1920s, argued that

The existence of a force called Public Opinion is in the main taken for granted, and American political writers have been most interested either in finding out how to make government express the common will, or in how to prevent the common will from subverting the purposes for which they believe the government exists (1922).

In the 1950s and 1960s, the idea that public opinion shapes American foreign policy behavior was largely rejected by political scientists; as one writer summed up the prevailing view: "The evidence suggests that the day-to-day conduct of foreign policy by the executive branch is almost completely unrelated to general public opinion" (Hughes 1978: 107). Opinion surveys seemed to reflect a profound public ignorance with regard to foreign affairs (Lerche 1967: 120); furthermore, such surveys indicated that opinion tended to follow the initiatives of foreign policy leaders (cf. Cohen 1957; Schneider 1974).

Many recent studies have challenged these findings. First, the extent to which policy elites are insulated from public opinion appears to have been greatly overstated. Page and Shapiro (1983) studied 357 cases of significant policy changes between 1935 and 1979; in 66 percent of those cases, the changes were congruent with public opinion. Studies by Monroe (1979) indicate that the consistency between opinion and policy is particularly evident for foreign policy and other "highly salient" issues. Second, in a high percentage of cases, changes in policy follow rather than precede changes in public opinion. As Page and Shapiro conclude: "When American policy preferences shift, it is likely that congruent changes in policy will follow" (1983: 129).

How can we make sense of these varied findings on the relationship between public opinion and foreign policy? Much depends on the way public opinion is conceptualized. Daniel Yankelovich

(1979) argues that public opinion needs to be understood in terms of a configuration of values which impose constraints on policymakers. These values set the parameters for what the public will accept in foreign policy. On different issues at different times, they set the boundaries of the possible for foreign policy leaders; no policy which consistently disregards popular goals can maintain the legitimacy necessary for implementation.

How, then, can public opinion shape policy? In essentially three ways. First, whether revealed through scientific surveys or unscientific counting of letters and phone calls, public opinion can shape policy through elected officials' fears of the public. As Destler et al. (1984) argue, presidents and congressmen often, in effect, create the public attitudes that constrain them—that is, they often perceive public demands and constraints as stronger than they are, and formulate policy with a careful eye on the potential public response. The evidence for this is largely anecdotal, but it heavily colors most memoirs dealing with the processes of high-level policymaking. Most politicians are acutely aware of the potential consequences of widespread public dissatisfaction with their leadership.

The second way public opinion can shape policy is through voting—the threat of "electoral punishment." One of the more convincing recent theories of congressional behavior begins with the assumption that "congressmen are single-minded seekers of reelection." As Mayhew puts it, the electoral goal "has to be the proximate goal of everyone, the goal that must be achieved over and over if other goals are to be entertained" (1974). The brevity of congressional terms and the increasing cost of campaigning reinforce this focus (cf. Smith 1988). For a president, if his immediate policy concerns generally override his concern with reelection, there is nevertheless an immense coterie of appointees aware that their positions depend on his reelection or the election of a suitable successor. The importance of foreign policy issues in determining electoral outcomes has become increasingly evident in recent years; presidential elections in 1968, 1972, and 1980 revolved to a considerable extent around foreign policy issues. Even traditional bread-and-butter issues like inflation and unemployment are increasingly foreign policy issues; much of the public is becoming aware that economic prosperity depends on competitiveness in foreign trade (Yankelovich and Harmon 1988).

Third, public officials draw on public opinion as a resource in internal policy battles—that is, competing factions within the elite attempt to evoke favorable public opinion to strengthen their policy claims. As one writer puts it:

> In periods of policy conflict, the faction of the elite that can command popular support for its cause—or that can marshall enough evidence to make a claim for the existence of such support—will be well-placed to dictate the terms of a new foreign policy consensus (Sanders 1985: 136).

Public opinion is an important resource for conducting elite struggles,* and taking foreign policy issues into the public realm can help to resolve bureaucratic and political conflicts within the government.[†]

Finally, the so-called "attentive public"—those with the greatest interest in foreign affairs—tends to make itself heard through organizations. It is often misleading to speak of "public influence" in general; as one high official in the State Department puts it, officials pay little attention to public opinion, but are constantly barraged by "publics, concerned not with foreign policy in general, but with specific issues."** As Michael Leigh states in his work on the opinion constraint in foreign policy: "As an amorphous set of attitudes distributed among the population, public opinion is neither accessible nor germane to the policy process. It can enter the process only when crystallized, articulated, and 'submitted' to those involved in the formulation of policy" (1976). This "submitting" of public opinion to policymakers, of organizing values into political objectives so that they can attain status on the foreign policy agenda, is increasingly performed by foreign policy advocacy groups. We

*Interview with Charles Hill, executive assistant to former Secretary of State George Shultz, Washington, 26 July 1988.

[†]Former Reagan White House Communications Director David Gergen has been quoted as saying that "everything here is built on the idea that the President's success depends on grassroots support" (see Kernell 1986).

**On the notion that politics frequently involves an increase in the "scope of conflict," see Schattschneider (1960).

will consider next the role of these groups in contemporary American foreign policy.

ADVOCACY GROUPS

Lobbying groups have long been a central concern of writers on American politics. David Truman is most closely identified with the concept that the policy agenda is defined by the political pressures coming from organized interests in society. He conceives of the political process as one in which the role of government is to mediate among various societal demands as represented by the claims of competing interest groups: "Both the forms and functions of government are a reflection of the activities and claims of such groups" (1951: 505). Government serves largely as a mechanism for facilitating adjustments worked out among competing group claims.

The interest-group pluralist conception of politics—that there can be no single interest of the nation which transcends the interests of its constituent groups—has long been rejected by students of foreign policy. Whatever the ambiguity of the concept of "national interest," it is hard to conceive that certain irreducible interests such as physical survival, national freedom, and economic subsistence can fail to be seen as collectively shared interests (cf. George and Keohane 1980). Nonetheless, beyond consensus on these minimum interests, the competition among groups representing competing values in the foreign policy arena is increasingly approximating the processes of domestic politics.

"Whenever ideologies seem to be important in politics," observes Barnes, "they have a firm organizational basis" (1966). For the last two decades, the organizational basis for ideological demands has increasingly been advocacy/pressure groups, think tanks, and other organizations designed to influence opinion and policy. Foreign policy lobbies are by no means a new phenomenon in the United States. In the immediate post–World War II period, for instance, lobbying efforts to influence foreign policy came not only from business, labor, and ethnic groups, but also from a wide range of ideologically motivated groups—religious, women's, and veterans' organizations, as well as more extreme groups from pacifists on the left to ultra-nationalist groups like the so-called China Lobby on the right (Cohen 1957). In the 1950s and 1960s the China Lobby was the quintessential example of an ideologically motivated amalgam of groups exercising virtual veto power over a sphere of U.S. foreign policy (Schurmann 1974: esp. 169–83). Since the Vietnam War the number and influence of organized groups acting in the foreign policy arena has grown dramatically. Though recent figures are clearly distorted by tougher contemporary reporting requirements, the total number of lobbyists officially registered with Congress has increased from 365 in 1961 to over 23,000 in mid-1987 (Smith 1988: 29). The foreign policy lobby comprises not only a growing number of specific interests with increasingly international concerns—e.g., business groups, labor, farmers, etc.—but also an increasing number of ideological advocacy groups. For example, there are currently 70–80 groups, many connected with churches, concerned solely with influencing American policy on the single issue of human rights violations in the Third World (Schoultz 1981). The pro-Israel lobbying groups, the anti-nuclear movement organizations, various pro-military lobbies, and networks of think tanks and political action committees on both the right and left maintain a constant flow of information and demands directed at Congress, the White House, the State Department, and the news media.

The emergence of substantial, well-organized lobbies as major channels of ideas and values impinging on the policy process is one of the more significant developments in post-Vietnam foreign policymaking. State Department officials observe that the growth of issue-specific advocacy groups and organized public opinion on key issues has become an "immense barrage."* Advocacy groups are most evident in issues which are prominent on the current agenda of American foreign policy—apartheid in South Africa,† Israel and the Palestinian question (cf. Blitzer 1985; Rubenberg 1986: Ogene 1983), Central America and the issue of American intervention abroad,**

*Interview with Hill.

†Cf. Metz (1986); also interview with Eric Benjaminson, Assistant Southern Africa desk officer, State Department, Washington, 26 July 1988.

**Interview with Heather Foote, Washington Office on Latin America, Washington, 30 July 1988.

arms control and the nuclear arms race (Waller 1987), and facets of foreign economic policy (Aggarwal et al. 1987).

A significant feature of contemporary foreign policy advocacy groups is their dependence on domestic public opinion. Organized pressure groups can draw on "insider" or "outsider" tactics in their efforts to influence policy. Insider tactics involve using contacts inside the Administration, the State Department, or Congress to shape the foreign policy agenda. Personal friendships, recognized expertise, and established working relationships are the currency of insider tactics.* Outsider tactics generally involve bringing issues to the attention of a larger public to increase pressure on legislators (Schattschneider 1960: 257). Skilled use of the mass media to focus attention on issues is the chief outsider resource. As David Truman argues, propaganda is a crucial tool for pressure groups seeking to mobilize public opinion. By using the channels provided by the mass news media, pressure groups can challenge the once nearly exclusive ability of the president to define foreign policy issues to a national audience.

Another significant feature of contemporary foreign policy debates is the prevalence of ideologically motivated groups driven by value concerns rather than by interest calculations. Advocacy groups on the left like SANE-Freeze or the various groups backing Nicaragua's Sandinista government, and think tanks like the Institute for Policy Studies, are motivated primarily by shared ideologies; on the right, a network of groups from Jerry Falwell's former Moral Majority to the Committee on the Present Danger to think tanks like the Heritage Foundation are similarly held together by common value concerns. The ideological nature of contemporary foreign policy advocacy groups explains the importance of outsider tactics. While both left and right advocacy groups also use traditional insider methods of influence, their ability to mobilize large constituencies on key issues is their major resource. The Committee on the Present Danger, for example, which was formed in 1976 to oppose continued detente with the Soviet Union, was effective in part because of the insider

*Interviews with Lindsay Mattison, executive director, International Center for Development Policy, Washington, 25 July 1988; Kim Holmes, Heritage Foundation, Washington, 30 July 1988; and Heather Foote, Washington, 30 July 1988.

status of its members, but chiefly because it was instrumental in pushing public opinion to a more hawkish stance on detente, defense spending, and the desirability of the SALT II arms control treaty (Sanders 1983). On the left, nuclear freeze advocates acquired clout only to the extent that they spurred a widespread, grass-roots movement which later found many congressional backers (Waller 1987). Anti-apartheid activists have mobilized supporters, particularly on college campuses, and human rights advocates have drawn on an influential religious constituency; in each case their influence has depended on the constituencies they were able to mobilize throughout the country.

Advocacy groups, then, have emerged in the foreign policy process as the central link between values and policy. They serve to infuse policy ideas with those values, and to submit them to decision-makers. As a result they are the most significant channel of public pressure on foreign policy-making.

LEADERSHIP: CONGRESS AND THE PRESIDENT

The significance of advocacy groups and public opinion can only be measured by their impacts on foreign policy leadership. Since Vietnam the role of leadership—turning values and ideas into policies—has increasingly been contested between the president and Congress. In the cold war era, the president had acquired, with the tacit consent of Congress, virtually complete foreign policy responsibility. Bipartisanship in practice often meant nonpartisanship; foreign affairs and national security were deemed too important to be buffeted by political dissensus. The apogee of foreign policy bipartisanship was reached with the Gulf of Tonkin Resolution in 1964, and has been in decline ever since, most dramatically in the early 1970s. Since the closing days of the Vietnam War, Congress has vigorously asserted its constitutional role in overseeing (and occasionally even formulating) foreign policy (Crabb and Holt 1980).

This growing foreign policy role of Congress since Vietnam has been noted—and lamented—by many observers (cf. Vogler and Waldman 1985; Franck and Weisband 1979; Sundquist 1981). While the president retains the initiative in designing and implementing policy, presidential authority is no longer unassailable; members of Congress have publicly challenged the president's authority to define the national interest, which they rarely if ever did in the 1950s and 1960s. In certain instances—such as sanctions against South Africa and the decision to withdraw American support for Ferdinand Marcos in the Philippines—Congress has in fact initiated policy shifts. More often it has played a reactive role, but by bringing foreign policy debates into the more open arena of Congress, it has helped decentralize policymaking authority.

What is the basis of Congress's post-Vietnam willingness and capability to act in foreign policy matters? The U.S. failure in Vietnam was the catalyst that helped precipitate dramatic changes in the congressional foreign policy role. The breakdown of policy consensus created a new willingness by members of Congress to test the limits of presidential authority. A series of reforms instituted in the 1970s enhanced congressional capability to influence foreign policy: the increase in staff resources, particularly for junior members, has given senators and congressmen access to the information and expertise needed to challenge the president on foreign policy issues (Muskie et al. 1986). The declining authority of committee chairmen and senior congressmen and senators, part of the general breakdown of congressional hierarchy, has left younger members freer to pursue their own agendas, which increasingly include foreign policy issues (Polsby 1986). In short, as Congress became more decentralized and more democratic, it became more effective in influencing foreign policy. As a result, in the 1970s Congress played a major role in shaping policy on such issues as the Panama Canal treaties, arms sales to the Middle East, the trade embargo of Rhodesia/Zimbabwe, and the evolution of arms control with the Soviet Union. Congress also asserted authority over American covert operations by vetoing intervention in Angola in 1975 and by enhancing efforts to control the CIA (Bennet 1978).

Institutional changes in Congress have been reinforced by other factors. First, with developments in Vietnam, foreign policy suddenly acquired a significant electoral dimension. Congress is a quintessential elective culture: the preeminent goal for legislators is reelection, and as a result they are highly responsive to constituents' attitudes

(Mayhew 1974; Smith 1988). Advocacy groups, trained in the techniques of political organizing and pressure, have been able to use greater public concern over foreign policy as a lever to persuade legislators to challenge the president on foreign policy issues. Foreign policy political action committees funnel campaign contributions directly to legislators who support certain stands on foreign policy issues—or to challengers who oppose those stands. Second, the personal convictions of senators and congressmen appear to have shifted as well. Some of this reflects a reaction to Vietnam; much of the shift has resulted from the dramatic influx of new members in the last decade. The younger politicians, like the constituencies they represent, are increasingly partisan and ideological (Nathan and Oliver 1983). Finally, the media has played a crucial role in transforming the Senate from what Nelson Polsby called "an inward-looking, intensely parochial men's club to a publicity-seeking hothouse of policy initiation and self-promotion" (1986: ix). Through access to the media, legislators have increasingly been able to carve out public roles for themselves outside the restrictions of the institutional framework; many senators and congressmen have acquired national stature on foreign policy issues which enables them to challenge presidential authority.

Generally speaking, the resurgence of Congress has had two major effects on policymaking. First, it has increased the impact of public opinion and advocacy groups in formulating and/or obstructing foreign policy. Congress has always been more susceptible than the executive branch to well-organized lobbying efforts, and ideological movements spearheaded by advocacy groups succeeded in influencing Congressional policy on the rejection of the SALT II treaty, the blocking of aid to the Nicaraguan contras, the call for a nuclear freeze, and the imposition of sanctions against South Africa. The willingness of Congress to challenge presidential prerogatives on foreign policy has opened a new channel for ideological demands; rather than dealing with an unsympathetic president or State Department fiercely resistant to lobbying pressure, advocacy groups can frequently find a sympathetic ear in Congress.

Second, the resurgence of Congress has in certain ways redefined presidential foreign policy-making. The ability of Congress to make foreign policy issues "public" has forced presidents to make stronger cases for their foreign policy programs (Kernell 1986) and made it more difficult to legitimate policy. Much of Reagan's success in implementing his foreign policy goals can be traced to his effectiveness in mobilizing public opinion. (Conversely much of Carter's failure can be traced to his ineffectiveness.) Skillful use of the media is increasingly a prerequisite for the effective exercise of foreign policy authority. Somewhat paradoxically, the resurgence of Congress has also increased presidential incentives for running covert policies. The Iran-Contra affair can be traced to this new environment of foreign policy-making. In the absence of a congressional consensus for aid to the contras, the executive branch attempted to provide support in secret. Its exposure, and the severe political fallout which resulted, underscore the danger of bypassing the process of foreign policy consensus building. As Douglas Bennet, Jr. has stated, the resurgence of Congress "implies that the pace at which America adjusts to new global realities will not be much faster than the public consensus can move" (1978).

In this chapter we have examined the value cleavages in American political culture with regard to foreign policy, and the channels through which ideological demands are brought to bear on foreign policy-making. In the next chapter we will consider more specifically three key symbolic issue-areas—nuclear weapons and arms control, human rights, and intervention—to see how ideological politics have shaped policy.

Chapter 3

THE PEOPLE AND FOREIGN POLICY:
CASE STUDIES

INTRODUCTION

The impact of ideological politics is most significant on a relatively small number of key symbolic issues which raise questions that are crucial for the legitimation of foreign policy. By "symbolic" issues we are referring not to those which lack substance, but rather to those which develop a significant public constituency and are evocative of the larger concerns underlying a nation's foreign policy and its position in the world. The key symbolic issues of modern American foreign policy—the nuclear arms race, relationships with communist nations, human rights, intervention in the Third World, the relationship with Israel and policy in the Middle East—have also been among the most substantial. From our perspective, three aspects they share are particularly noteworthy. First, they are constantly accessible to the "attentive public" through the mass news media. Second, they are generally broad policy issues, which are significant enough to garner public attention, but not pressing enough to require crisis decisions at the highest levels of government; they thus offer both incentive and opportunity for public input (cf. Zimmerman 1973; Cohen 1957). Finally, these issues evoke the larger principles underlying foreign policy, raising powerful moral as well as interest considerations. The legitimacy of a state's foreign policy—the extent to which it commands popular support—rests less on the mundane details of its diplomatic or economic performance than on its handling of these key symbolic issues.

There is an analogy here to the workings of a parliamentary system of government. In a parliamentary system, the government falls when it loses a vote in the legislative body on an issue considered crucial to the right of the government to remain in power. Not every vote of parliament is considered an issue of "confidence"; votes on minor issues can be lost without the government being obliged to call an election. But major votes on the budget, key foreign policy initiatives, crucial campaign promises, etc. are considered issues of confidence, and a loss by tradition obliges the government to step down.

Similarly, in the American system certain foreign policy issues are crucial for the legitimacy of the government's broad foreign policy aims. Notable examples are the American decision to go to war with Spain in 1898; the controversy over American participation in the League of Nations following World War I; the crisis in Greece and the proclamation of the Truman Doctrine by the U.S. government in 1947. In each of these cases, the ramifications of the decision went far beyond the particular issue involved: they legitimated broad policy programs which defined the country's approach to foreign affairs—its conception of the "national interest."

Which issues become important symbolic ones, and why, is more difficult to answer. Cobb and Elder, who have done perhaps the most significant work on this question, concede that "Contemporary political science perspectives are unable to . . . explain how a previously dormant issue can be transformed into a highly salient political controversy" (1983). Whether issues will acquire what they call "agenda status" is an outcome of interactions among interest and advocacy groups, legislators, the executive or other decision-makers, the mass media, and the general public. The growing influence of the mass media in structuring popular perceptions and interpretations is central to this process: their "agenda-setting" power gives them the collective capability of turning sometimes secondary issues into issues of legitimacy—the recent Iran-Contra scandal in the United States being a prime example.*

Issues are more likely to acquire symbolic status when political elites are divided over policies; such divisions mean that politics of bargaining and compromise among the executive, the legislature, and the bureaucracies are less likely to succeed. Policy cleavages increase

*On the notion that the mass media play a crucial role in setting political agendas, see esp. Cohen (1963), McCombs and Shaw (1972), Erbring et al. (1980), Gitlin (1980), and Tuchman (1978).

the incentive for both sides to "expand the scope of the conflict" (Schattschneider 1960), to carry the issue to a larger audience. Symbolic issues are also most likely to emerge in times of uncertainty when previous policies are no longer perceived as able to cope with new challenges (Leigh 1976).

When foreign policy issues become symbolic, their resolution, and hence the direction taken by foreign policy, will be the product primarily of internal political forces rather than the constraints of international politics.* In other words, the outcome will depend primarily on how effectively public opinion and group pressures are translated into political power through legislative channels. As Michael Leigh observes, in such situations "the formulation of foreign policy occurs within a domestic context whose imperatives often appear more salient to the policy-maker than those of the international situation" (1976: viii). In the discussion that follows, we will argue that this convincingly explains a number of recent developments in American foreign policy.

I. NUCLEAR WEAPONS AND ARMS CONTROL

The existence of nuclear weapons is often seen as one of the strongest arguments against a public, or even congressional, role in foreign policy-making. The need for firm presidential control over decisions regarding the use, deployment, and force structure of America's nuclear arsenal is generally considered axiomatic (Lifton and Falk 1982). After 1945, the potential use of such destructive weapons was quickly recognized as not only the central issue of superpower politics, but indeed as the central political issue confronting all mankind. In the context of the cold war, it was easy to argue that the potential "irrationalities" of democratic politics, and especially of ideological politics, have no place in an arena where the cost of miscalculation could be catastrophic.

Since the early 1970s, however, it has proved increasingly difficult for presidents to keep the nuclear issue out of the public realm.

---

*This argument is made with regard to domestic politics by Cobb and Elder (1983: 163).

The ritual incantation of national security interests has not been sufficient to stifle domestic controversy over the implications of nuclear weapons for international politics and American foreign policy. On the anti-nuclear left, for instance, activists have seen in the "revitalization of democracy" the only hope for preventing the people from destroying themselves; as E.P. Thompson writes, "A prior condition for the extermination of peoples is the extermination of the open democratic process" (1982). The nationalist right, while historically more interested in military control of nuclear weapons than in popular control, has frequently invoked public opinion in policy battles over deployment decisions. Its struggle against communism abroad has been conducted in considerable part through a struggle for public support at home.

How can we evaluate the role that ideological politics—the political clash of values and ideas—has played in the formation of recent American nuclear policy? On the one hand, because nuclear weaponry is highly technical and complex, experts are accorded large policy roles. Much of the debate over nuclear deterrence and warfighting doctrines has been the province of an elite circle of civilian and military strategists—Fred Kaplan's "wizards of Armageddon" (1983). Beginning with Bernard Brodie's seminal writings, academic theorizing has frequently exercised a direct influence on American nuclear doctrine (cf. Brodie 1959; Schelling 1985–86). The language of missile accuracy, survivability, and throw weights reveals a debate not easily accessible to the uninitiated, but nuclear weapons policy has powerful ideological dimensions as well. Robert Levine (1987) points to the essentially theological nature of the nuclear debate, and Joseph Nye has argued that "much of what passes for nuclear knowledge rests on elaborate counterfactual argument, abstractions based on assumptions about rational actors, assumptions about the other nation's unknown intentions, and simple intuitions" (1987). The parameters of the nuclear debate have been set as much by faith as by expertise, and as in any faith, the authority of the priests rests in good measure on the convictions of the followers.

As an ideological issue, the divisions over nuclear policy are clearly evident. Since Hiroshima, the left and right have been deeply split over the meaning of nuclear weapons for global politics and

American foreign policy. While both sides are concerned about American security, they differ radically over what this entails. For the left, the advent of the atomic bomb undermined the notion that security resides in military strength and national sovereignty (Katz 1986). The belief that security had ceased to be a national concern and become a global concern extended beyond the pacifist fringe into segments of the liberal establishment. War would have to give way to other means of resolving international disputes; aggressive nationalism would have to give way to cooperative internationalism. These arguments were adopted by many of the scientists who had worked on the first atomic bomb, most notably J. Robert Oppenheimer,* and the postwar efforts to create international control of atomic energy through the Baruch Plan, largely originated by Oppenheimer, developed out of this cluster of values and beliefs. In recent years a vigorous anti-nuclear movement calling for arms control, mutual disarmament, or even unilateral disarmament has been a consistent factor in the nuclear debate. Advocacy groups from SANE-Freeze to the American Friends Service Committee to the Physicians for Social Responsibility have succeeded in keeping the issue of disarmament on the public agenda.

For the right, on the other hand, there has never been any question that American nuclear predominance is the key to American security. The bomb was seen as the weapon which would make America invulnerable (a quest rekindled by Ronald Reagan's Strategic Defense Initiative). As William F. Buckley, Jr. rhapsodized: "We view our atomic arsenal as proudly and as devotedly as any pioneer ever viewed his flintlock hanging over the mantel as his children slept and dreamed" (quoted in Kolkey 1983: 124). If Buckley's rhetoric was unique, his sentiments were not: many agreed from 1945 on that the primary purpose of the bomb was the military defense of the United States. This was the basis of the nationalist demands that operational control of nuclear weapons be turned over to the military.† To the

*On the role of the scientific community in the early debates over nuclear weapons, see York (1975).

†The efforts of the nationalist-military alliance to place operational control of nuclear weapons under the military are discussed in Schurmann (1974: esp. 83–91).

right, the lessons of Munich had been clear: nuclear dominance and military readiness would bring security; weakness would invite attack. Demands for nuclear superiority, warfighting capabilities, and a vigorous opposition to arms control have been central to their platform.

Nuclear weapons and arms control are clearly a crucial symbolic issue in American politics. The issue of nuclear war is one which has galvanized more grass-roots response—in such forms as protest marches, disarmament petitions, and nuclear-free-zone ballots—than any other foreign policy issue. We posited earlier that when foreign policy issues acquire symbolic status, their resolution is likely to reflect the balance of domestic forces more than the constraints of international politics.* Pollsters Daniel Yankelovich and John Doble (1984: 35) have offered convincing evidence that the shifts in America's nuclear policy since the early 1970s, from detente/arms control to containment/arms buildup and back again—can be traced more to internal American politics than to Soviet actions. Policy shifts from confrontation to conciliation in almost cyclical fashion have reflected the ability of competing elite groups to capture public opinion. The changes in policy have tended to follow rather than precede changes in public opinion, indicating the sensitivity of policymakers to domestic shifts on the nuclear issue.

Public opinion has been a significant weapon for ideological groups of both the left and right. In the late 1970s and early 1980s, both were able to use public opinion effectively. First, the right mobilized opposition to the SALT II treaty, and later the left mobilized support for a nuclear freeze and the resumption of arms control talks.

---

*The argument over "internal" versus "external" causes of foreign policy change is often a futile one. As Robert Putnam has said: "Domestic politics and international relations are often somehow entangled, but our theories have not yet sorted out the puzzling tangle. It is fruitless to debate whether domestic politics really determine international relations or the reverse. The answer to that question is clearly 'Both, sometimes'" (1988). One can argue that external events influence policy depending on how they are filtered through domestic politics. Thus the collapse of detente in the late 1970s, for instance, can be seen not as a direct response to the Soviet invasion of Afghanistan, but as a result of the interpretation President Carter, other policy leaders, and the general public put on the Soviet action.

The reason both right and left ideologies have been able to draw on public opinion has to do with the complex character of that opinion. The values of the American public on nuclear issues are, as Schneider (1987) has pointed out, multi-dimensional. Like the ideological right, much of the public tends to distrust the Soviets, seeing them as expansionist, aggressive, and likely to interpret conciliatory and friendly gestures as signs of weakness, and public opinion therefore consistently rallies behind a policy of military strength (Sussman 1988). Yet much of the public is increasingly worried about the possibility of nuclear war and determined to contain the arms race and avoid open confrontation. As Schneider has argued, the public wants both strength and peace. The evolution of American nuclear policy can be traced in part to the alternating dominance of these two perspectives within the mass public. When fears of Soviet strength and American weakness are dominant, the right is able to draw on widespread public support. When, on the other hand, fear of nuclear war is dominant, the left commands public backing.

The influence of ideological politics in shaping nuclear policy was less evident before the early 1970s. U.S.-Soviet negotiations leading to the 1963 partial test ban treaty and to the 1972 ABM treaty were almost completely insulated from congressional oversight or direct public pressure. To be sure, public concern over nuclear fallout from atmospheric testing in the 1950s and fear of nuclear war triggered by the Cuban Missile Crisis contributed to the 1963 treaty (Jensen 1988: 88–92), and Congress eventually played a role during ratification of the SALT I treaty, particularly with the passage of the Jackson amendment in 1972. That amendment, which followed extensive and often critical congressional scrutiny of executive arms control policy, called for ongoing "policy guidance" from Congress and for numerical missile equality in any subsequent U.S.-Soviet treaties. Before the 1970s, however, public interest in the nuclear issue was limited enough that advocacy groups had little success mobilizing followers and Congress felt little constituent pressure to play a more active role in policy formulation (Platt and Weiler 1978).

How can we account then for the emergence of ideological politics in the realm of nuclear policy? Two factors in particular seem important. The first is a gradually growing public awareness of the potential consequences of nuclear war. Whether through the general expansion of education, the growing influence of the mass news media (particularly television), or the successful campaigns of advocacy groups, Yankelovich and Doble (1984) find that public concern over nuclear weapons has increased substantially. In 1955, for instance, only 27 percent of the people polled by Gallup believed an all-out nuclear war would lead to the destruction of mankind; by 1984, 89 percent thought it would. Polls taken in 1984 showed that almost 75 percent of the population found themselves thinking more about the possibility of nuclear war than they had five years previously. By the 1980s nuclear policy had entered the public consciousness and become an issue with potential electoral consequences.

The second crucial factor is the breakdown in the 1970s of the policy consensus between left and right which had sustained presidential control of nuclear policy (Fascell 1987). The components of this consensus can be examined by looking at the Nixon administration's policy. Nixon's multi-dimensional detente strategy—arms control and peaceful coexistence coupled with continued U.S. Soviet rivalry in certain weapons systems—accorded well with the often conflicting public attitudes on the nuclear issue. Congressional acquiescence was guaranteed largely because the policy generated little political opposition. As Yankelovich and Doble observe: "Such is the nature of public ambivalence toward the Soviet Union that it dooms to failure any one-dimensional policy that appeals exclusively to one side of public attitudes" (1984: 43).

Later presidents who ignored this lesson helped to rupture the policy consensus, making themselves vulnerable to the pressures of ideological politics. Nixon had walked the delicate line between right and left, but Carter and Reagan both strayed and were pushed back, less by the force of external events than by the pressures of domestic politics. Carter's efforts to secure ratification of the SALT II treaty were undermined by the ideological right; Reagan's efforts to delegitimize arms control negotiations were overridden by the ideological left.

Carter, who attempted to push the Nixon detente agenda ahead by continuing the SALT process, unfortunately lacked Nixon's right-wing credentials. He ran into the concerted opposition of organized right-wing groups, who succeeded in building public opposition to the SALT II treaty (Scheer 1982; Sanders 1983; Barnet 1981). Why should this have been so, since in most important respects SALT II followed in the footsteps of SALT I, merely restraining arms expansion rather than reducing armaments? While Carter accurately perceived the public desire for arms control, he misread the public mood on the issue of military strength. By the time he took office in 1976, news stories were already emerging to the effect that the Soviets had taken advantage of detente and the SALT I treaty to seek superiority in nuclear weapons.* The accuracy of these claims has been much debated (cf. Pipes 1977; Garthoff 1978), but throughout his presidency Carter was confronted with charges of declining American and rising Soviet power which, reinforced by events in Iran and Afghanistan, ultimately led to the demise of SALT II.

The role of advocacy groups in consolidating public opposition to SALT II was vital in undermining Senate support for the treaty. Leading the fight was the Committee on the Present Danger (CPD), a group of powerful ex-government officials, business leaders, academics, and journalists opposed to Carter's military policy, many of whom subsequently joined the Reagan administration. During the SALT II hearings, CPD members testified 17 times, participated in almost 500 television or radio programs, distributed over 200,000 pamphlets, and wrote scores of articles in conservative journals and daily newspapers (Barnet 1981). The CPD relied heavily on public opinion to enhance their influence, and were primarily responsible for taking the arms control debate out of the hands of diplomats and technical experts and into the public arena. The CPD's campaign was quintessentially ideological and played on public fears that America's supposed military weakness invited aggression (CPD 1976/77). That their message got through seems clear: public opinion favoring increased military spending, which hovered between 7 and 17 percent during 1969–1974, had by March 1980 reached an astonishing 76 percent (Russett and Deluca 1981). The failure of

*Cf. "New CIA Estimate Finds Soviet Seeks Superiority in Arms," *New York Times*, 26 December 1976, and "World Military Situation Confronting Carter Shows Changes Have Favored Soviet," *New York Times*, 4 January 1977.

SALT II ratification was primarily a result of this loss of domestic backing.*

While the Reagan administration's nuclear policy in its early years benefitted from the public rejection of SALT II, it also foundered on its inability to forge policy consensus between left and right. If Reagan correctly gauged the public mood favoring military strength, he ignored—until well into his second term—the extent to which the public feared nuclear weapons and favored their negotiated control or reduction. While polls indicated that huge majorities thought nuclear war with the Soviets was unwinnable, top Reagan officials casually bandied about theories of limited and winnable nuclear war (Gray 1979; Scheer 1982), and while the public continued to clamor for negotiations with the Soviets, Reagan officials questioned the possibility of successful arms control (Talbott 1984). Virtually all of Reagan's early political appointments were men concerned with building weapons, not limiting them.

Much as the right wing used organized advocacy groups to oppose Carter's policies, the nucleus of left-wing opposition to the Reagan policy lay in similar networks of activists. The idea of a bilateral nuclear freeze, which became the policy proposal galvanizing both public and congressional opposition to Reagan's nuclear policy, emerged from the network of anti-nuclear groups such as the American Friends Service Committee and SANE-Freeze (Garfinkle 1984). Even more than the campaigns of the right wing, which relied heavily on the support of religious fundamentalists, the freeze movement was a grass-roots campaign. Its tactics were centered around local freeze resolutions, mailing campaigns, and mass rallies. In June 1982, over one million people rallied in New York to support arms reductions or disarmament—the largest single antiwar rally in American history (Katz 1986). Organized anti-nuclear groups, working with supporters in Congress, in August 1982 came within two votes of passing in the House a resolution calling for a bilateral freeze on

*The failure of SALT II ratification has frequently been attributed to the Soviet invasion of Afghanistan, but Senate support for SALT had declined well before the Soviet invasion. The failure of SALT seems more directly connected to internal politics (which was shaped by Soviet behavior in the 1970s) than to any specific international events.

the development and deployment of nuclear weapons; the resolution was finally passed in amended form in May 1983 (Waller 1987). Much as the right had taken the nuclear issue to the public, and concentrated its political lobbying efforts on Congress, so the left adopted similar tactics. The result, if perhaps not as immediately effective as the anti-SALT II campaign, was to keep nuclear weapons and arms control on the public agenda, forcing an administration suspicious of arms control to resume negotiating with the Soviets. The freeze resolution was ultimately less important for what it contained than for what it symbolized—a broad public opposition to the nuclear policy of the early Reagan years.

It seems clear then that many of the policy oscillations of recent years can be traced to the vagaries of ideological politics. This would appear to bear out fears that ideological competition results in inconsistent and incoherent policies. The shifts of American policy indicate the instability which can arise when foreign policy issues become public issues. Yet U.S.-Soviet strategic relations appear to be in better shape today than at any time since the outbreak of the cold war. Much of this is attributable to Gorbachev and the "new political thinking" in the Soviet Union; in the last four years, the Soviet Union has clearly seized the initiative in proposing new arms reduction measures. Nonetheless, it was the United States which first broke out of the stagnant SALT process—a process which in many ways had served only to legitimate the growth of a more accurate, more destabilizing missile force. While President Reagan's initial claim that the only sort of arms control he was interested in involved deep reductions in forces seemed in many ways hypocritical, it became a formula for uniting the domestic right and left on the nuclear issue.

If the ideological right helped to undermine SALT, the resumed American interest in arms control in the late Reagan years was influenced by the anti-nuclear left, which pushed the Administration to reenter serious negotiations. And the left brought with it a demand for much more serious steps toward disarmament than had ever been considered under the SALT process.

The signing and ratification in 1987 of the Intermediate Nuclear Forces (INF) treaty—the first treaty to actually eliminate a whole class of existing weapons—appears to represent a revival of the early 1970s arms control consensus, though in many ways at a much deeper and more fundamental level. In recent public polls, 55 percent of the public approved strongly of the Reagan-Gorbachev START formula aimed broadly at reducing by half the number of strategic range nuclear weapons; another 27 percent favored it somewhat (Beatty 1989: 59). Among key members of Congress, and the elite policy circles of academic experts and government officials, there is a similarly strong consensus in favor of arms control.

The earlier policy consensus, while it accorded with public opinion, was never based on actively solicited public support. The INF treaty, in contrast, represents a domestic compromise arrived at through a struggle between the right and the left, each with its bureaucratic supporters, congressional allies, influential advocacy groups, and plausible claim to represent a significant portion of public opinion. The accord accepts the right's claim that relative military strength must be safeguarded, and that intrusive verification is necessary to ensure treaty compliance, while accepting the left's arguments about the continuing need for a negotiated end to the arms race. No more evidence of consensus is needed than the fact that only three senators voted against the treaty—the strongest congressional support ever for an arms control accord.

It is by no means clear, then, that the ideological conflict of left and right has undermined sound policy. We would argue, rather, that the evidence is that this conflict has served to stabilize and strengthen policy. Ideological conflict helped to push the arms control process along new and potentially more beneficial paths, as well as to legitimate the changes among a broader populace. On the nuclear issue, then, ideological conflict has produced a new consensus.

II. HUMAN RIGHTS IN AMERICAN FOREIGN POLICY

Even more clearly than the issue of nuclear weapons, the emergence of human rights on the American foreign policy agenda underlines the inadequacy of seeing foreign policy behavior as purely interest-based. The notion that one state has a right, even an obligation, to interfere in the affairs of another sovereign nation on behalf of the victims of human rights violations is an idea that can in no way be derived from traditional realpolitik concepts. As George Kennan writes:

> The interests of the national society for which government has to concern itself are basically those of its military security, the integrity of its poli ical life and the well-being of its people. . . . Whoever looks thoughtfully at the present situation of the United States in particular will have to agree that to assure those blessings to the American people is a task of such dimensions that the government attempting to meet it successfully will have very little, if any, energy and attention left to devote to other undertakings, including those suggested by the moral impulses of its citizens (1985/86: 206–7).

Despite the realist admonitions, the issue of human rights has acquired a central place on the agenda of American foreign policy. The idea that all people should be free from arbitrary arrest, imprisonment, and torture by their governments has, of course, powerful moral resonance. As president, Jimmy Carter made human rights the symbolic cornerstone of his foreign policy; Ronald Reagan initially rejected the human rights thrust as part what he saw as the failed policies of the detente era, but popular and congressional pressure forced the issue back on the policy agenda. American policies toward South Africa, the Soviet Union, the Middle East, the Philippines, and Latin America continue to be shaped in part by human rights concerns. The salience of human rights has not been a result primarily of interest concerns, though many have argued that American interests are served by defending rights abroad (cf. Feinberg 1983). Whatever the interest ramifications, America's human rights policy originated not from interest concerns but from values: it is a product of ideological politics.

U.S. policies to protect human rights have taken two basic forms. The first is expressions of disapproval directed at countries guilty of consistent human rights violations. Quiet diplomacy is the most common American approach, used often by both the Carter and Reagan administrations. Public diplomacy, aimed at bringing "world opinion" to bear against offenders, was resorted to frequently by

Carter, though under Reagan it was used primarily against the Soviet Union and its allies. It is also the tactic underlying the State Department's annual "country reports," which list in detail human rights violations around the world. The second approach is to adopt direct sanctions against offending states by reducing or withdrawing military and/or economic aid. This has been the tactic advocated by Congress since the mid-1970s. Such a policy is necessarily limited to those states receiving American aid. The Carter administration employed sanctions in a number of cases, including the postponement or elimination of aid for Nicaragua, Afghanistan, and Ethiopia, reduced assistance to such countries as El Salvador, the Philippines, and Chile, and the termination of military sales to Argentina (Mower 1987: 103). The Reagan administration originally tried to reverse the policy of linking American aid to human rights performance, but by its second term had restored much of the policy.

The problem with all of these approaches is that they potentially conflict with other foreign policy goals—e.g., shoring up friendly governments, preventing the emergence of unfriendly governments, or maintaining cordial relations with other sovereign states.* The human rights issue is thus particularly susceptible to value cleavages, because it conflicts directly with other policy ends. While all Americans agree in principle with the goal of protecting human rights abroad, they are sharply divided about its desirability as a central tenet of foreign policy.

The human rights issue is thus deeply problematical for American foreign policy. For the last two decades, government policy has fluctuated, alternatively reflecting opposing sets of values. Polls show that the public as a whole remains confused, that support for human rights policies has not been reconciled with the concern for protecting American economic and security interests (Russett and DeLuca 1981). Value cleavages between left and right are strong, bureaucratic battles divide the State Department, and policies fluctuate depending on

*The State Department and its ambassadors have traditionally been resistant to human rights policies for this reason. An active human rights policy, which involves criticisms, often public, of the internal behavior of other sovereign states, is seen as undermining the cordial state-to-state relationships necessary for effective diplomacy (see Mower 1987: 67-81).

which constituencies exercise greater influence on the Administration and Congress. The lack of a policy consensus makes human rights one of the more consistently divisive issues on the foreign policy agenda.

To what extent is the human rights policy a product of domestic ideological politics? To answer this question, we must examine the three components of ideological politics—values, political ideas, and leadership.

In terms of values, the issue of human rights ultimately deals with how people define their community—how they decide who is "inside" and who is "outside" the community. The American right wing, very much in the conservative tradition, has tended to take a narrow view of what constitutes the community. As Rousseau (1967) argued, human loyalties are naturally strongest in small groups; society can be seen as a series of concentric circles in which one's family forms the strongest bond of loyalty and commitment, followed by one's neighborhood or town, and finally by one's nation. Conservatives, while embracing progressively more inclusive communities, have historically drawn sharp lines between insiders and outsiders. They wish to see individual rights—as laid down in such documents as the American Bill of Rights and the French Declaration of the Rights of Man—guaranteed for those inside the community. But for outsiders, different rules apply. The right insists that concern for human rights must be subordinated to the defense of the community (cf. Falk 1981). Their preferred policy has been to ignore human rights issues wherever they potentially interfere with geopolitical or economic interests. When the right has denounced human rights violations, the charges have been almost exclusively directed against the Soviets and their allies and have reinforced security-based policies. This position is by no means an extreme one; public opinion surveys indicate little support for a policy that promotes human rights abroad at the expense of American national security interests (Schoultz 1981: 25).

Left ideology, in contrast, is based in part on the denial of the insider/outsider distinction as relevant for policy. The ideas of the left emerge out of a natural law tradition, reaching back to Grotius and Pufendorf, which starts with the postulate of human sociability and derives from this the existence of international norms and responsibilities binding on all nations (Hoffmann 1981: 13). The idea of a "global community" or "one world" figures prominently in left rhetoric. Human rights violations are seen, therefore, as a global concern, not simply a national one. The left supports a human rights policy as an end in itself. While public support depends very much on the value trade-offs in relation to other goals, the left position enjoys considerable popular backing: both "mass" and "elite" opinion have consistently favored American efforts to pressure countries which violate human rights—if necessary by withdrawing American support from human rights violators (Oldendick and Bardes 1982: 398).

For the left as well as for the right, human rights has frequently been used to strengthen other policy goals. In the early 1970s, for instance, the left denounced human rights violations primarily to reinforce arguments against American intervention in Vietnam and Chile. In contrast, the left avoided criticizing violations in the Soviet Union for fear this might jeopardize East-West detente (Cohen 1977). The 1974 Jackson-Vanik amendment, in which Congress linked U.S.-Soviet trade to the emigration of Soviet Jews, was championed by the right wing in Congress.

Until the early 1970s, America did not have a human rights policy. Despite occasional rhetorical concern, there were no institutions or policies explicitly aimed at defending human rights abroad. Yet by the end of the 1970s, the United States had officially made American military aid contingent on human rights performance, had injected human rights criteria into multilateral lending, and had established a substantial bureaucracy in the form of the human rights bureau of the State Department.

The policy responded to both domestic and international developments (Crahan 1984: 19). The most important domestic factors were the civil rights movement and the resurgence of Congress's foreign policy role; the most important international factors were the Vietnam War and the growing focus on American support for authoritarian regimes in the Third World, most particularly the military junta which overthrew the elected government of Salvador Allende in Chile in 1973 (Drinan 1987: 73). The former provided the organizational and moral basis for human rights demands; the latter provided the rationale.

The civil rights movement was the domestic precursor of the human rights policy. The interest components of the civil rights movement—the problems of poverty and social breakdown—were much less salient than the value components, the reaction against perceived injustice. The chief demand of the civil rights movement was that the rights of membership in the political community be extended fully to black Americans.

The human rights foreign policy was initially an extension of the values and ideas of the civil rights movement (Schoultz 1981; Metz 1986). The human rights lobby that emerged in the 1970s adopted both the goals of the civil rights movement—the increasingly broad protection of basic human and civil rights—and the tactics—the populist effort to bring moral outrage to bear on the policymaking process. This was done chiefly by advocacy groups, which collaborated with various members of Congress to redefine the place of human rights in American foreign policy.

Before 1973, with the Vietnam War still lingering, the human rights lobby was virtually nonexistent. In the 1970s, however, it emerged as one of the larger, more active foreign policy lobbies (Schoultz 1981). The reasons for this explosion of activity are numerous: many groups, such as those opposed to apartheid in South Africa, had roots directly in the civil rights movement; others were part of the anti–Vietnam War movement, which, with the revelations in 1969 of the My Lai massacre, had in part become a protest against American human rights violations in Vietnam; still others were formed following reports of U.S. covert operations in Chile which contributed to the overthrow of the Allende government and to the escalation of human rights violations there. Many were religiously backed organizations which drew on the moral influence of the churches to bolster their case. Finally, a number of organizations were formed later in direct response to the Reagan administration's early efforts to emasculate the human rights policy.

There are basically two sorts of human rights advocacy groups (Weissbrodt 1981). The first, composed of groups like Amnesty International, Americas Watch, and the International Committee of the Red Cross, stay aloof from direct lobbying activities. They concentrate their efforts on objective reporting of human rights violations worldwide and on pressuring human rights violators through extra-governmental channels. The second, composed of groups like the Washington Office on Latin America and the various organizations opposing apartheid, concentrate on direct political activity—in particular, lobbying Congress for changes in American policy.

One of the clearest examples of the influence of the human rights lobby is the success of the American anti-apartheid movement. The core of that movement is a trio of advocacy groups—the American Committee on Africa, the Washington Office on Africa, and Trans-Africa. The fight against apartheid is an excellent example of interests confronting values in American foreign policy. Despite substantial U.S. economic and security interests in South Africa, American policy has become increasingly value-driven. In the 1970s and 1980s advocacy groups focused their efforts on persuading Congress to enact a comprehensive package of economic sanctions against South Africa. Crucial to the success of this effort was their ability to mobilize public opinion. In 1984 the Free South Africa Movement, which organized demonstrations on college campuses across the country, played a key role in putting the apartheid issue on the front burner of the foreign policy agenda (Sussman 1988: 178–83). Despite the efforts of the Reagan administration to pursue quiet diplomacy in the form of "constructive engagement" with South Africa, in preference to a policy of vigorously opposing apartheid, popular pressure channelled through Congress pushed American policy toward more comprehensive sanctions. In 1985 Congress approved a limited package of sanctions against South Africa. In October 1986 this was expanded to include a ban on the import of iron, steel, uranium, coal, textiles, and agricultural products from South Africa; a ban on exports of petroleum products and nuclear equipment to South Africa; and the prohibition of new American investments in South Africa. Most recently, in August 1988, Congress approved, over the opposition of President Reagan, a comprehensive sanctions package including a ban on most exports to and imports from South Africa, disinvestment, and prohibitions on military cooperation.

The strength of the human rights policy is attributable finally to leadership, and it is there that the ideological struggle over the policy is most evident. While there have been no "anti-human rights" advocacy groups, many conservatives in Washington have consistently opposed the human rights thrust. As with the nuclear arms issue, members of Congress and successive administrations have vied to lead public opinion on the human rights issue. The liberal-left in Congress initially played the leading role. Beginning in 1973 the Subcommittee on International Organizations of the House International Relations Committee, chaired by Donald Fraser, held regular hearings on human rights violations abroad. This led directly to a series of policies passed by Congress over the opposition of Presidents Nixon and Ford—the most significant being the 1974 amendment to the Foreign Assistance Act which ordered the president to "reduce or terminate security assistance to any government which engages in a consistent pattern of gross violations of internationally recognized human rights" (Boettcher 1981; Drinan 1987). Other congressional initiatives called for the establishment of a human rights bureau in the State Department, mandated annual reports on human rights violations, and tied certain foreign aid programs to human rights concerns (Mower 1987: 61).

Each of these initiatives was strongly opposed by the Administration. Secretary of State Henry Kissinger argued in 1973 that "it is dangerous for us to make the domestic policy of countries around the world a direct objective of American foreign policy" (quoted in Drinan 1987: 75). He later refused to comply with congressional demands that the State Department report on the human rights records of nations receiving aid.

It was Jimmy Carter who in 1977 first began to use executive authority to support the human rights policy. Carter brought with him strong personal religious and moral commitments, and was determined to reestablish foreign policy on a more idealistic footing, to root it in the country's "moral values." He also clearly recognized the political value of making human rights the rhetorical and symbolic centerpiece of his foreign policy (cf. Drinan 1987: 82). Without Carter's support, it is unlikely that the injection of human rights concerns into American diplomacy would have survived the intense hostility from existing bureaucratic interests, particularly from the regional bureaus of the State Department (Mower 1987: 67–69). Carter's 1977 appointment of Patricia Derian, an outspoken human rights advocate, as the first assistant secretary of state for human rights and humanitarian affairs ensured that human rights would no longer be overlooked by the State Department.

Carter's concern for human rights by no means ignored geopolitical calculations. Within the Administration there was an ongoing struggle between Secretary of State Cyrus Vance and national security adviser Zbigniew Brzezinski which mirrored the value cleavages between left and right. In cases where American security interests were clearly at stake—Iran, China, South Korea, the Philippines, and Indonesia—Carter opted for geopolitics over human rights, refusing to antagonize important allies with charges of human rights violations (Mower 1987: 61). What the Carter policy did, however, was create a human rights bureaucracy, complementing the support coming from Congress and from advocacy groups on the left.

The extent to which human rights had become entrenched in American foreign policy became evident only when the Reagan administration tried to dismantle the policy. In the 1980 election campaign, Reagan vigorously denounced the Carter human rights policy as a failure, asserting right-wing values which subordinated human rights to the larger struggle against the Soviet Union and communism. He embraced Jeane Kirkpatrick's (1979) argument that if America refused to support "authoritarian" human rights violators like Somoza in Nicaragua, this would lead to the spread of Soviet-backed "totalitarian" regimes. In his first news conference as Reagan's secretary of state, Alexander Haig asserted that "international terrorism will take the place of human rights in our concern because it is the ultimate of abuses in human rights" (quoted in Drinan 1987: 95). The appointment of Elliott Abrams as assistant secretary for human rights and humanitarian affairs in 1981 indicated the Reagan administration's equation of human rights with staunch anti-communism, and in its first months it urged Congress to reinstate military aid to four countries—Chile, Guatemala, Argentina, and Uruguay—which had been denied assistance for human rights violations.

While Reagan attempted to subordinate the human rights issue to the cold war struggle with the Soviet Union, he was unable to eliminate it entirely: he faced not only an entrenched human rights bureau in the State Department, which grew throughout his term in office, but also the continued existence of advocacy groups with links to the Congress and a substantial public constituency favoring human rights policies.* When the Administration's efforts to derail the human rights policy failed, what emerged was an ideological struggle —frequently pitting the president against Congress—over when and where to press countries for human rights improvements. The Administration focused its efforts on countries such as Nicaragua, using human rights to reinforce anti-communism, but it was forced repeatedly to justify its failures to denounce egregious violators such as Turkey and Guatemala (Jacoby 1986).

By 1986, however, in one of the dramatic turnarounds that characterized his presidency, President Reagan was promising to "oppose tyranny in whatever form, whether of the left or the right" (quoted in *ibid.*: 1067). His decision to embrace the human rights policy he had once denounced was not merely rhetorical. As early as the latter half of 1983, in the face of congressional threats to cut off military aid, the Reagan administration was pressuring El Salvador to improve its human rights record, and in 1986 it withdrew support from two long-time American allies with deplorable human rights records—Ferdinand Marcos in the Philippines and Jean-Claude Duvalier in Haiti.† Perhaps most significant in the long term for American foreign policy, human rights has acquired a major place on the agenda of Middle East policy. Apparent Israeli complicity in the refugee camp slaughters in Lebanon in 1982, coupled with the televised violence of Israeli soldiers during the Palestinian *intifada* in 1988–89, have made human rights a major issue in American support for Israel.

What do these various measures concerning human rights add up to? In the last two decades human rights policy has been a consistently

*The strength of the human rights community was demonstrated in 1981 when Reagan's first nominee to head the Human Rights Bureau, Dr. Ernest Lefever, was rejected 13–4 by the Senate Foreign Relations Committee. Lefever, who had argued that human rights concerns had no place in diplomacy, was vigorously opposed by human rights advocacy groups.

†President Reagan was forced to withdraw support for Marcos largely through the efforts of Senator Richard Lugar and others in Congress who drummed up domestic opposition to him. However, the U.S. decision to back Corazon Aquino ultimately had more to do with Marcos's apparent weakness than with his human rights violations (see Bonner 1987).

controversial item on the foreign policy agenda. Introduced against presidential opposition, the policy has been buffeted by ideological struggles between the left and right. As Tamar Jacoby has observed:

> To an outsider, this public disputation often seemed unnecessary and distracting—a needlessly ad hominem and bitter controversy for controversy's sake. Yet on other occasions it seemed to serve a useful purpose, conferring new legitimacy on human rights issues and providing the noisy background clamor—the evidence of domestic American concern—that was often needed to give some meaning to the administration's quiet diplomacy (1986: 1082).

Ideological politics, in other words, have been essential for building legitimacy for a human rights policy and for convincing other states of the seriousness of the American concern.

There are indications that this ideological turmoil has led toward an emerging consensus on human rights. Both left and right acknowledge the seriousness of human rights violations worldwide, and both are less inclined to use the issue cynically as a pretense for advancing other policy goals. At the same time, adversaries like the Soviet Union and many East European states have admitted to human rights violations and taken steps to reduce them. The place of human rights discussions in U.S.-Soviet summitry is evidence both of the weakening of "inviolable" national sovereignty and of the strengthening of international norms.

Despite this, however, the ideological cleavages over whether the United States should pursue an activist human rights policy remain deep. Human rights policies are in essence interventionist; by emphasizing the existence of norms and responsibilities which transcend national borders, they raise fundamental questions about the role of the nation-state in world politics and about the role of American foreign policy in the future world order.

III. THE POLITICS OF INTERVENTION

The question of intervention—under what conditions, and for what political ends, should the United States interfere in the internal affairs of sovereign nations?—is perhaps the most volatile issue in contemporary American foreign policy. American domestic opposition generated by the failure of intervention in Southeast Asia lingers to this day in the so-called "Vietnam syndrome"—the public's unwillingness to see U.S. military power engaged in Third World conflicts. Even supposedly covert forms of intervention, like American aid to the Nicaraguan contras, have been subject to intense public scrutiny: the congressional debates over intervention in Central America have been the most ideologically charged foreign policy debates of the 1980s. Whatever American interests may be at stake in the Third World, the issue of whether America should intervene in support of those interests has become enmeshed in ideological politics.

Intervention is a costly policy for states to pursue: it denies what Hedley Bull has called the fundamental ethic of international society—i.e., the mutual recognition of national sovereignty—and frequently angers friends and enemies alike.* Yet intervention has historically been among the special rights and/or duties accorded to great powers in international politics: the right to intervene to control crises, restrain allies, limit wars, or maintain spheres of influence has long been considered axiomatic in great power politics (Bull 1977).

Intervention as understood in international law and United Nations texts refers to direct, coercive interference by one state in the internal affairs of another. Hoffmann defines intervention by states as "acts which try to affect not the external activities, but the domestic affairs of a state" (1987). Intervention overtly challenges national sovereignty by using the power of one state, or a collective of states, not to alter the foreign policies of another state, but to alter its internal behavior (most conspicuously its type of government). In the nineteenth and early twentieth centuries, such intervention took both economic and military forms—from European colonialism in Africa and Asia to the recurrent American incursions in Latin America. In

---

*This was clearly demonstrated by the refusal of America's NATO allies, except for Great Britain, to support the U.S. raid on Libya in 1986 launched in retaliation for Libyan terrorist activity. With the possible exception of encouraging the overthrow of the South African government, the positions taken by Third World nations in the United Nations have been entirely anti-interventionist (see Bull 1984).

the late twentieth century, following the post-World War II demise of colonialism, overt military intervention has been increasingly replaced by covert intervention and by various forms of economic interference, but it remains a central tool of foreign policy.

By its very nature, intervention involves the actions of great powers in smaller states. For the United States, intervention primarily concerns its relationship with the ex-colonial world—a problem that has bedevilled recent American foreign policy more than any other. As Charles Maynes (1988: 117–18) points out, conflicts in the Third World—Korea, Cuba, Vietnam, Iran, Nicaragua—have stained the foreign policy records of every postwar president. American policy in the Third World has continually run up against the limits of foreign aid and of military power to dictate internal politics even in small countries.

Repeated U.S. failures in the Third World tend to belie any simplistic equation of domestic consensus with foreign policy effectiveness. Through much of the cold war (until at least the late 1960s), administrations enjoyed a strongly pro-interventionist foreign policy consensus. The containment policy consensus with regard to the Third World rested on two pillars: first, the belief (by the right, in particular) that communist governments in the Third World were a threat to U.S. security interests and ought to be prevented from coming to power, and second, the belief (by the left/liberal wings) that non-communist, preferably democratic, governments were the best hope for generating economic modernization and political liberalization. This linkage of American security and moral/humanitarian concerns was one of the central bases of foreign policy bipartisanship.

Within the parameters of the containment policy consensus, intervention was seen as a tool for maintaining the American sphere of influence and preventing the expansion of Soviet-backed communist regimes. Many of the examples of American overt intervention in the cold war era—Korea during 1950–53, Lebanon in 1958, the Dominican Republic in 1965, Indochina during 1965–73—were cases in which the United States was defending friendly regimes from a feared communist takeover (Girling 1980: 142–43).

There was a second current, however—American covert intervention—operating largely outside the parameters of the containment consensus, which played a crucial role in interventions in the 1950s and 1960s. The influence of right-wing values and beliefs inside the military and the Central Intelligence Agency took operational form in covert attempts to "roll back" existing communist regimes. CIA involvement in the overthrow of governments in Iran in 1953, Guatemala in 1954, and Chile in 1973, as well as the ongoing covert war against China in the 1950s and early 1960s, were all attempts to roll back communism (Schurmann 1974: 161–68, 404–16). Thus American interventionist policy followed essentially two approaches: one was an overt policy aimed at maintaining friendly governments; the other, a covert policy aimed at destabilizing unfriendly ones.

In the late 1960s and early 1970s, domestic opposition to the Vietnam War both weakened the containment consensus and challenged the covert activities of the military and the CIA. First, American support for corrupt and illegitimate South Vietnamese governments highlighted contradictions between the two pillars of containment policy. It became evident that many "friendly" Third World leaders— Marcos in the Philippines, the shah in Iran, Somoza in Nicaragua— were guilty of gross human rights violations and had minimal domestic legitimacy. Both the wisdom and morality of the American preference for stable authoritarian regimes over unstable democratic regimes came under increasing scrutiny (Feinberg 1983). Thus the moral/humanitarian dimension of American interventionism came into increasing conflict with the national security dimension, and the policy consensus of the cold war era could not be sustained.

Covert activity was also subject to intense scrutiny following Vietnam. The Pentagon Papers had revealed the seemingly inexorable process by which covert commitments led to overt military involvement, and congressional critics of the CIA role in overthrowing the Allende government in Chile (the Church committee) acted to cut off covert aid to Angola in 1975 (the Clark amendment) in attempting to prevent a reoccurrence. Many major institutional changes were made by Congress in the 1970s in an effort to assert some control over covert operations; they included the 1974 Hughes-Ryan amendment requiring the president to report to select congressional committees concerning all CIA covert operations, the creation of Senate and House intelligence committees, and measures requiring disclosure of arms sales and secret agreements (Sharpe 1988).

The weakening of the containment consensus and the hostility toward covert action has meant that the United States has, since Vietnam, lacked a widely accepted doctrine of intervention. There is little national consensus over whether, or for what ends, intervention is justified. Policy has fluctuated from issue to issue, depending largely on the coalitions which can be built between the Administration and Congress. As Alexander George has written: "In the absence of the fundamental consensus that policy legitimacy creates, it becomes necessary for the President to justify each action . . . on its own merits rather than as part of a larger policy design and strategy" (1980). The intervention issue is the classic case of policy conducted without a stable consensus in the face of sharp domestic ideological divisions.

As with the issues of nuclear weapons and human rights, domestic values and ideological cleavages are crucial to explaining recent American intervention policy. The resilience of the "Vietnam syndrome" is demonstrated in public unwillingness to support any but the most costless interventions in conflicts abroad (Schneider 1983), but this anti-interventionism does not indicate a reemergence of American isolationism. Opinion polls show continued support for a global American role, up to and including military intervention under a fairly wide range of circumstances (Russett and DeLuca 1981). Many of those who oppose military intervention for security reasons favor interventionist tactics on human rights or other issues. For example, American economic sanctions against Panama in 1987, made in an attempt to oust General Manuel Noriega because of his connections to drug trafficking, generally won popular support despite failure to oust the general. What is at issue for public opinion is a twofold question: first, under what circumstances is intervention justified, and second, what role should military force play in interventionist policies?

These questions reveal sharp ideological cleavages at both elite and mass levels. Left and right are polarized over such crucial issues as the status and desirability of U.S. hegemony abroad, the role of the CIA, the threat posed by Third World liberation movements, and the morality and/or utility of relations with Third World dictators (see Mandelbaum and Schneider 1979; Holsti and Rosenau 1984).

Ideological conflict revolves around the question of whether the Third World should be seen primarily as a battleground for U.S.-USSR proxy wars, or as a separate sphere of foreign policy necessitating goals distinct from the U.S.-Soviet conflict (Maynes 1988: 118). The right continues to support intervention, including covert and overt military intervention, in overseas conflicts deemed threatening to American security interests; the left opposes the use of military force except against the most immediate threats to national security, but it continues to support interventionist pressure on behalf of human rights and self-determination in the Third World.

Intervention has been a central ideological issue for the American right. Unlike much of the liberal-left, the right feels comfortable with military force, and finds its strongest institutional supporters within the military services. Right-wing values and ideology frequently acquire a doctrinal and operational basis in military strategy. What are the values which give right ideology a base in popular constituencies? Most fundamental is "patriotism," which has become a kind of codeword of support for the military. Patriotism implies the vigilant defense of the nation against outsiders. Indeed it often shades over into subtle and not-so-subtle forms of jingoism and racism—the fear of the "other" which has loomed so large in American political culture (see Rogin 1987). Reagan's appeals for public support of U.S. aid to the Nicaraguan contras, for instance, drew frequently on such themes as the looming "Soviet threat," the alleged Nicaraguan role in funneling drugs into the United States, and the potential for a flood of refugees and illegal immigrants if more communists came to power in Central America (see Kenworthy 1987).

As an ideology, the right has linked the cluster of values associated with patriotism with a particular theory of intervention which has a number of distinct dimensions. First is the argument, which appears to have originated with Maxwell Taylor, that the cold war between the West and the East will be won or lost in the Third World. Nuclear armaments preclude direct conflict; therefore, the balance of power will be measured by the tally of allies and enemies worldwide. Central to this argument is the domino theory and the idea that the battles crucial to American national security will be fought far from American soil: failure to stem communist advances abroad will ultimately lead to American decline (Gaddis 1987). Nothing has weak-ened the right's belief in the need for "forward" defense, and the lessons of Munich still hold sway—i.e., failure to respond to threats shows a weakness of will which only encourages further enemy aggression.

The position of the left is more complex and paradoxical. It is tempting to argue that the left is simply anti-interventionist, but it is evident that on issues of human rights, poverty, and various forms of injustice, the left sees a need for intervention. The idea of inviolable national sovereignty is not one of the left's sacred values. The extreme anti-interventionist position taken by some on the left has been hard to maintain—it works best if one equates intervention with injustice, as writers like Noam Chomsky (1973) are inclined to do concerning American interventions. In the wake of the Vietnam War, the anti-in-terventionist stance was extremely strong on the left and contributed significantly to the isolationist themes of the McGovern candidacy in 1972. However, a much larger segment of the left tends to distinguish between interventions that are detrimental and interventions that are beneficial to the countries affected. They might support economic aid while opposing military aid, or support intervention on behalf of victims of human rights violations while opposing intervention in support of anti-communist insurgents. The left on the whole has refused to rule out intervention as a legitimate tool of American foreign policy.

What the left has sought to rule out in all but the most extreme circumstances is *military* intervention. Attitudes toward the military may be the best indicator of an individual's position on the left-right spectrum. The left—from moderate liberals to non-Marxist radicals—is strongly opposed, both emotionally and intellectually, to the use of military force. Some of this opposition is connected with religious pacifism, but much of it arose from the experience of the Vietnam War, which led many observers to conclude that the projection of American military power exacerbated rather than solved global prob-lems, often contributing to human rights violations. The left, there-fore, almost categorically refuses to support American military intervention in the Third World.

How have these ideological divisions influenced recent American policy with regard to intervention? The clearest test case in recent years has been in Central America, particularly U.S. policy toward El Salvador and Nicaragua. The influence of ideological politics is especially evident here because of the limitations of interest-oriented explanations. For instance, Jeane Kirkpatrick's claim that "Central America is the most important place in the world for the United States today" (quoted in LaFeber 1983: 5) must be seen as a purely ideological evaluation. Tangible American interests in the region are negligible: in geopolitical terms, it is marginal compared with the Middle East, Japan, or Western Europe;* Central American raw materials are strategically insignificant compared, for instance, with South Africa (Girling 1983: 191); even the Panama Canal, no longer large enough for modern warships, is becoming obsolete. Economically the region is also unimportant to the United States, representing less than half of one percent of American private profits from foreign direct investment (*ibid.*).

Despite this minimal strategic and economic importance, Central America became the most controversial region for American foreign policy in the 1980s. The Reagan administration was able to overcome ideological divisions and carve out a reasonably stable policy consensus on El Salvador, but on Nicaragua such consensus proved elusive. As a result, the Administration turned to clandestine operations, concealed both from Congress and the public, to carry out its Nicaraguan policy. The subsequent Iran-Contra scandal underscored the difficulties and political costs of trying to conduct policy in secret.

The situation in El Salvador in the late 1970s and early 1980s—a military-civilian junta faced with an indigenous communist insurgency—fell within the framework of the old containment consensus. As Cynthia Arnson (1988) argues, the ideological divisions on El Salvador were over means, not ends. Both left and right in Congress

---

*Quoting Margaret Daly Hayes: "The assumption that the United States has security interests in the region has never been questioned by the defense community. . . . [Yet] in the context of the strategic balance, Latin America has been only marginally important. The countries of the region have had little power, and the region has been generally isolated from global political and military conflicts" (1982: 86–87).

opposed the insurgency, but they differed over how to contain it. The right by and large accepted the so-called Kirkpatrick thesis, which posited a distinction between authoritarian states, which might one day become democratic, and totalitarian states, which never could. Thus, Kirkpatrick (1979) argued, the United States should support dictators like Somoza [authoritarians] rather than risk the emergence of Marxist [totalitarian] governments in the hemisphere, with grave national security implications. This was a thesis the left never accepted. Throughout the 1980s the liberals in Congress made their support of aid to El Salvador conditional both on evidence of an improved human rights record and free elections (McNeil 1988); by the end of 1983, evidence of human rights violations in El Salvador led to U.S. aid being cut in half by Congress (Arnson 1988: 41), despite the efforts of the right within the Administration.

A policy consensus which allowed a continued U.S role in El Salvador was the result primarily of the 1984 election victory of José Napoleon Duarte over a strong right-wing candidate. Duarte was the type of leader who made consensus possible: as a reformist who promised to improve the human rights record, he appealed to the left in Congress, and as an anti-communist who was willing to allow the Salvadorean military free rein in conducting its war against the insurgents, he appealed to the right in both Congress and the Administration. Leaders like Duarte and the Philippines' Corazon Aquino—moderate, yet staunchly anti-communist democrats—may be the only type of leaders who can produce a stable, pro-interventionist coalition in the United States. It remains to be seen if this consensus can survive the coming to power of the right-wing ARENA party in El Salvador. The consensus behind Duarte and Aquino revealed a new sort of thinking in the 1980s about the type of governments the United States should support. Simple anti-communist credentials no longer suffice: democratic elections and a positive human rights record are increasingly prerequisites for American backing.

On Nicaragua, however, as noted earlier, consensus proved elusive. Between 1982 and 1986, Congressional votes on aid to the Nicaraguan contras switched no fewer than six times, fluctuating from support for generous aid packages to a complete prohibition on all but "humanitarian" assistance (Kissinger 1987). Throughout the

Reagan years, left and right in the United States could find no middle ground over Nicaragua. To the right wing, Nicaragua represents an implacable communist enemy in the midst of the U.S. sphere of influence. It became the testing ground for the revival of cold war rollback policies institutionalized in the Reagan Doctrine and in the strategy of low intensity conflict (LIC).

The evolution of LIC reflects an attempt by the right to revive counter-insurgency policies discredited by the Vietnam War. LIC doctrine sees the U.S.-Soviet conflict evolving primarily in the struggle for the allegiance of Third World states. Through military assistance to friendly governments, support of anti-communist insurgencies, anti-terrorism and anti-drug operations, LIC envisions the use of both military and non-military intervention to counter Soviet influence in the Third World (see Klare and Kornbluh 1988: 55–56). The most visible component of the Reagan Doctrine has been the effort to roll back communist regimes by supporting anti-communist insurgents. In 1987 American aid to insurgents totalled $250 million to the Afghan *mujahidin* fighting the Soviets, $100 million to the Nicaraguan contras, $15 million to Jonas Savimbi's UNITA guerrillas in Angola, and $3.5 million to anti-Vietnamese guerrillas in Cambodia (Bernstein 1987). In total, American aid in the form of weapons, military aid, and security-related economic assistance increased from $110 million in 1980 to over $800 million by 1985 (Guidry 1987).

Throughout Reagan's presidency, however, he could never sell a policy for LIC against Nicaragua to either Congress or the American public. The House's Boland amendment, which was first passed in 1983, restricted and finally halted aid to the contras, and expressed congressional refusal to allow the United States again to engage in covert attempts to overthrow foreign governments. Despite its occasional support for packages of "humanitarian" aid to the contras, Congress consistently opposed the Administration's war on Nicaragua; in so doing, it reflected deep public opposition to the Reagan policy of attempting to overthrow the Sandinista government (Leo-Grande 1987).

Unable to build consensus on a Nicaraguan policy, the Administration began to circumvent congressional funding cutoffs. Funds for the contras were raised from U.S. private citizens, foreign governments (such as Israel and Saudi Arabia), and arms sales to Iran (Kornbluh 1987). During the period when U.S. government aid to the contras was outlawed by the Boland amendment, the so-called Project Democracy supplied some $50 million to the contras, with a further $10–$30 million coming from Iranian arms sales (*ibid*.: 33). This was supplemented by humanitarian aid provided by networks of right-wing organizations and advocacy groups. This massive effort, which lasted until the Iran-Contra scandal broke in 1987, ultimately failed to sustain the contras as a fighting force or to create domestic support for overthrowing the Sandinistas. The scandal became the greatest policy fiasco of the Reagan years, and sharply lowered the president's standing with the American public.

American policy toward Central America in the 1980s reflects the strengths and weaknesses of policy made under conditions of ideological conflict in the absence of policy consensus. The strengths are primarily those of openness: the failure of the Administration to succeed in its covert policy is indicative of a level of congressional and public scrutiny missing in the cold war era. The sharp fluctuations in American policy, however, disrupted its relations with America's allies while clearly failing to improve the situation in Central America.

A new consensus on intervention does not appear likely, but we will consider some of the possibilities in our concluding section. American policy is caught in what may be the central paradox of global politics in the late twentieth century: on the one hand, an isolationist stance is increasingly unrealistic; on the other hand, the implications of intervention are increasingly uncertain. It is clear that the United States cannot turn its back on the rest of the world, in particular on the Third World; in an interdependent world, events abroad are crucial both for economic and security reasons, and the extension of humanitarian concerns (facilitated by a global mass media) means that people are less willing to ignore tragedy and suffering abroad. The potential for intervention increases as Third World states are wracked by internal strife, poverty, and human rights abuses. The challenge for American foreign policy is to build a broad domestic consensus around a policy that will serve both national needs and broader human concerns.

SUMMARY AND CONCLUSIONS:
FOREIGN POLICY IN A FLOODLIT SOCIETY

"Every diplomatist," the great British historian A. J. P. Taylor has observed, "dreams of independence":

> In an ideal world, he imagines, he would be pitted against the representative of a rival power as in a game of chess. He would be free to make his moves without anyone at his shoulder suggesting other moves or even forbidding the moves that he would like to make. Then, he supposes (quite wrongly), he would always win (1950: 354).

In contemporary democracies, he continues, not only is the chess player constrained by bureaucrats and legislators, but "the pawns assert the rights of 'the common man,' and insist on having the moves explained to them before they will move at all, and then often move in quite a different direction." In a similar vein, Bismarck, the quintessential practitioner of classical realpolitik, once lambasted the German Reichstag: "Foreign policy is difficult enough without three hundred asses trying to interpose their ill-formed opinions" (quoted in Waltz 1967: 9). The dilemma for contemporary foreign policy leaders is precisely how to make and implement policy in what Todd Gitlin has aptly termed "a floodlit society" (1980), in which the actions of leaders increasingly fall under the scrutiny of larger publics.

In the preceding pages we have argued that foreign policy in such a floodlit society is increasingly shaped by ideological pressures emanating from broad public constituencies. Under such conditions, foreign policy responds not only to external challenges and opportunities, but also to an array of internal pressures expressed through public opinion, advocacy groups, and legislators. On key symbolic issues, in particular—those which set the tenor of America's relations with the world—it is impossible to understand the contemporary dynamics of policymaking without reference to these ideological dimensions. The metaphor of international relations as a chess game played among relatively autonomous national leaders is inapplicable to most of the central issues on the foreign policy agenda.

Foreign policy has become an increasingly public, and ideologically contested, arena. There is every reason to believe that this "democratization" of foreign policy is not just a passing phenomenon, but rather a permanent feature arising from historical trends both internal and external to modern democracies. Internally, increased education and information have broadened the audience for international affairs. As one observer wrote almost seventy years ago, echoing a theme which goes back as far as the Enlightenment: "Education automatically widens the legitimate sphere of popular judgment; and when the mass of the voters comprehend the conditions of foreign policy there is no reason why they should not claim its control" (quoted in Waltz 1967: 11). Externally, the emergence of environmental issues, energy and resource issues, and many aspects of economic policy which blur the line between domestic and international affairs similarly expand the foreign policy constituency. Foreign policy concerns more people than ever before because it affects more people than ever before.

We have explored the impacts of ideological politics on policymaking, but the larger issue remains: what are the implications of this development for international relations in general, and for American foreign policy in particular? Can ideology and rational foreign policy, popular inputs and coherent outputs, be reconciled? What are the implications of democratically generated foreign policies for world order and the stability of relations among nations? Historically, as we have seen, the foreign policy records of democratic nations have been mixed. Democratically inspired policies have frequently been innovative and dynamic, but at other times have lacked the caution and moderation needed in world politics. What then is the future of global politics in what appears to be an increasingly democratic world?

IDEOLOGY AND POLICY

Many observers see in the growth of ideological politics a cause of the breakdown of foreign policy coherence and what they see as a crisis in policymaking. Faced with strong and frequently conflicting domestic pressures, policymakers are often forced to respond to demands which do little to further the pursuit of national interests in a complex and dangerous world. To pursue coherent goals, foreign policy-makers need to be insulated from ideological pressures, from the "excess of democracy" (see Nathan and Oliver 1983). It is our view, however, that democratic politics and ideological polarization, far from institutionalizing policy incoherence, are central to the formulation of clear and coherent policy. How can this be so? In evaluating America's foreign policy performance, Waltz has commented:

> One of the errors commonly made in assessing the merits of American government is to assume that because a series of pitched battles are fought within Congress and between Congress and the president, the policy that emerges must be as messy as the process by which it is made (1967: 109).

Ideological divisions which impress themselves on policymakers do create a messier, more conflictual policy process, but, as has been evident in the consensus emerging on nuclear weapons issues and in the strides made toward a clearer, more effective, and popularly backed policy on human rights and intervention, policy is more than the sum of the process by which it is made.

What is "policy"? Policy is essentially a course of action adopted by organizations to guide their activities. In the large-scale organizations of the state, policy is what moves the bureaucracies forward, what directs action. Policy, by its very nature, is made at the apex of an organization, but its impacts filter out to the society and the world through the various agencies of government. The essence of policy is anticipation—the projection of future developments and the creation of responses to deal with those developments. All policies propose something new—either new goals or new ways to achieve old goals. Policies either initiate change or are adopted as a response to change. They involve vision as well as adaptation. In other words, policies do more than simply respond on an ad hoc basis to changing circumstances (though ad hoc adjustments occur within the framework provided by policies); rather, they chart a course for the future, specifying goals and devising means for achieving those goals. That policies may frequently be frustrated by circumstances, and policy-makers forced to modify either ends or means in response to feedback from the policy environment, does not obviate the fact that policies are more than merely adaptive. They project a range of goals into the future and specify the means for achieving those goals.

The role of ideological politics in policymaking has frequently been overlooked. Policy involves change, and such change invariably conflicts with existing interests—both those of segments of society and those of governmental bureaucracies. Governmental organizations invariably tend toward routines. As Graham Allison has observed:

> To perform complex routines, the behavior of large numbers of individuals must be coordinated. Coordination requires standard operating procedures: rules according to which things are done. . . . At any given time, a government consists of existing organizations, each with a fixed set of standard operating procedures and programs (1971).

Policies which demand a change in these routines and programs inevitably conflict with the interests of bureaucracies, which is one reason why interest politics tend to play by the rules of the game. Bureaucracies concern themselves primarily with adjustment and stability: they engage in small adaptations of routines to deal with immediate threats or concerns. Larger adjustments do not emerge easily from bureaucratic environments.

One role ideological politics play in a democratic state is to shake up bureaucracies—to inject new policies and routines into governmental practice and to raise issues which might otherwise be overlooked or neglected. Ideological conflicts can raise larger questions of policy direction which would not emerge from a purely interest-oriented context. But where does support for new policies arise? How can politicians challenge entrenched interests and implement new programs of action? Both the impetus for change and support for change frequently come from ideological politics, from linking the values of broader constituencies with particular programs of political action. One of the major sources of policy innovation and change is the penetration of ideological politics into the routine operations of government. The revitalization of arms control, the pursuit of human rights abroad, and the reevaluation of interventionism emerged from the outside pressures of ideological demands, not from the workings of bureaucratic routine or the calculations of policy experts.

The limitations of an adaptive, purely interest-based foreign policy were recognized most clearly by E. H. Carr, whose writings are usually associated with a critique of moralism and utopianism. Despite his defense of political realism as an antidote to the utopian idealism of the interwar period, Carr argued that such realism was only half of what he called the "constant dialectic" of foreign policy. "Consistent realism," he argued, "breaks down because it fails to provide any ground for purposive or meaningful action (1939: 92)." Without finite goals, some emotional appeal, and a right of moral judgment—a politics of values, in other words—directed political action becomes impossible. The missing ingredient, which Carr called utopianism, and we have more conventionally called ideology, involves the "elaboration of visionary projects for the attainment of ends." By visionary, Carr did not mean unachievable, but rather a vision of policy which extends beyond the immediate, which sets goals for the future. Such ideologies are rarely attainable in the form articulated, and they probably would not produce good policies if implemented in that form. But they can serve to create political debate over new goals and to force a change away from stagnant or inadequate policies.

Ideological or value politics are essentially a politics of the future, creative rather than merely adaptive. They attempt to use the instruments of national policy to mold external conditions rather than simply to adapt to those conditions. In a world of flux, ideological politics are essential for pushing policies in new directions.

IDEOLOGY AND LEADERSHIP

We have written at some length about values and ideologies, but we have said considerably less about the third component in our tripartite structure of ideological politics—leadership. What is leadership? Peter Drucker, one of the more thoughtful commentators on the subject, argues that effective leadership involves "thinking through the organization's mission, defining it and establishing it, clearly and visibly" (1988: 16). We earlier discussed leadership in terms of the linking of popular values with particular policy aims. How can these two notions be reconciled? We agree with Drucker that the problem of leadership is fundamentally one of setting goals for an organization; in the case of foreign policy, this means directing coherently the actions of the relevant bureaucracies toward specified ends. The problem in foreign policy, as in all politics, is how to obtain political support for the exercise of leadership.

Foreign policy leaders, which in the United States means primarily the president and his closest advisers, have essentially three options in establishing their relationship with domestic constituencies. First, they can decide that foreign policy is simply too complex and dangerous to be exposed to any sort of mass pressure, and attempt to insulate policy from the vagaries of democratic politics. This was largely the strategy adopted by Nixon and Kissinger in their efforts to extricate America from Vietnam and to reorient the country's relations with the Soviet Union and China. Under certain circumstances, and with certain leaders, such an approach can be highly effective. In times of grave crisis in particular, power naturally flows to the top, and new policies may be demanded so urgently that they cannot wait for the process of domestic debate and compromise. Crisis, both abroad and at home, was the matrix which made possible Nixon's style of foreign policy leadership (Schurmann 1987). Such leadership, however, is not readily reconcilable with democratic politics under more normal conditions. The insulation of policy maneuvers from an aroused populace demands a level of secrecy and covert action, both internal and external, which may threaten the survival of democratic institutions. Nixon solved the foreign policy crisis of Vietnam, but was responsible for the domestic constitutional crisis of Watergate. What Nixon's leadership threatened to create was a presidential dictatorship, which no democratic country will tolerate except in a time of gravest crisis. Leadership which deliberately bypasses the institutions and mechanisms of compromise and consensus is antithetical to a society and political system based on democratic principles. In certain cases it may be necessary; rarely will it be tolerated for long.

A second strategy of foreign policy leadership, which accepts the fact that leaders need a solid political base if their policies are to succeed, involves the active effort to "sell" policies to larger constituencies. In American history this has tended to involve relatively simplistic and often highly emotional appeals to patriotic or crusading instincts (Hoffmann 1978). Governments have attempted to use such appeals to arouse support for, or stifle domestic opposition to, foreign policies. Theodore Lowi insists that since World War II the president and his elites "have been forced to oversell every remedy for world ailments and to oversell each problem for which the remedy might be appropriate"; such overselling attempts "to create the moral equivalent of war . . . for the purpose of imposing temporary and artificial cohesion upon the members of the foreign policy establishment" (1979: 174, 180). Classic examples include America's involvement in World War I, justified as the war to save democracy; the Truman Doctrine, which raised the specter of Soviet global imperialism; the Gulf of Tonkin resolution, which provided the immediate rationale for direct military involvement in Vietnam; and to some extent detente, which seemed to promise a profoundly transformed U.S.-Soviet relationship.

The use of this type of emotional advocacy, unlike the first style of leadership, takes seriously the need to build broadly based support for foreign policy. It recognizes that a policy not rooted in some appeal to values is unlikely to be sustainable in a democratic polity. Its problems are threefold. First, it tends to create unrealistic public expectations about foreign policy, which leads to subsequent disillusionment and popular backlash. The crusading spirit which led American soldiers into World War I inevitably turned to frustration when confronted with postwar realities, with the disastrous result that the country declined membership in the League of Nations. Similarly, the early, inflated hopes for detente were shattered by the continued expansionism of the Soviet Union. Second, this style of leadership tends to stifle debate over issues—to produce a kind of illusory consensus on values which prevents the consideration of alternative policies. Gelb and Betts (1979) argue that this sort of doctrinal consensus

contributed to the failure of the Vietnam policy by foreclosing alternatives and producing operational rigidity. Consensus by its very nature
circumscribes the issues and policy approaches considered legitimate
subjects of debate (cf. Partridge 1971). The problem with a consensus
built on highly emotional appeals is that dissent comes to be seen as
treasonous or unpatriotic. The third problem with this kind of leadership is that it does not lead to good foreign policy behavior. It encourages what Lowi (1979) calls "unambiguous acts"—displays of strength
or fortitude which may shore up domestic support, but which are "the
worst enemy of international diplomacy." The type of imperialism
associated with democratic governments emanates from this sort of
leadership; emotional appeals are rarely a good basis for subtle or
discriminating foreign policies. Many of the failures of the cold war
emanated from policy legitimated in part by emotional advocacy.
According to Stanley Hoffmann, "it would be perilous as in the past
to compress the necessary diversity [of foreign policy] into a few
simple moral slogans" (1978: 227).

The third style of leadership—the one we wish to advocate—
clearly lays out the goals and priorities of foreign policy for public
consideration, but is willing to modify both ends and means in the
context of domestic debate. Rather than hiding issues from the public,
or selling policies through highly selective public relations campaigns,
it should present issues to Congress, the media, and the public in
reasonably complete form. As Daniel Yankelovich has noted, based on
his experience in public opinion polling, public positions on key policy
issues tend to be as sophisticated as the debates among elites allow
(1979). Simplistic and emotional appeals frequently produce public
responses which are simplistic and emotional; a fuller, more complex
public debate leads to more articulate and informed public judgments.
Yankelovich's observations are confirmed by some of the issues we
have discussed here, in which public opinion, in the face of sustained
debates, has become sophisticated and nuanced. Leadership which
encourages such debate is likely to produce policy which is not only
supported domestically, but is also sufficiently complex and subtle to
respond to the realities of the international environment.

This is the kind of leadership which at its best characterizes the
discussion and resolution of purely domestic issues. Edward Banfield

(1986) has argued that domestic decision-making involves "social choice" as well as "centralized decision" processes. Central decisions are those made by an individual or small group acting on behalf of a larger constituency; social choice mechanisms, on the other hand, lead to decisions through a process of conflict and compromise among actors representing divergent interests or values. Central decision processes, Banfield argues, are fundamentally more "rational" in a technical sense—that is, in matching means to the pursuit of particular ends—but "the case for central decisions rests upon the assumption that it is possible for a competent and disinterested decision-maker to find in any situation a value premise that uniquely determines the public interest." More complex policy problems, those which invariably involve a wide range of interests and values, are more suited to social choice mechanisms which allow those interests and values to influence policy formulation.

Most writers on foreign policy have assumed that it is a sphere particularly suited to central decision processes. Leaders can pursue technical rationality, the matching of means to ends, because they possess a criterion—the national interest—which clearly defines those ends. But as we have argued here, and many others have argued before us, the concept of the national interest fails to provide an all-encompassing criterion for policymaking. Beyond certain "irreducible national interests"—which George and Keohane (1980) limit to physical survival, national liberty, and economic subsistence—the problem of conflicting values inevitably arises. For these sorts of decisions, which comprise most of foreign policy outside of immediate crises, some sort of social choice mechanism is necessary. Inevitably, as Banfield argues, central decision-makers will circumscribe the free interplay of conflicting values and interests, and actual decisions will reflect a mixture of the two processes. But what we are arguing for here in foreign policy decision-making is an expansion of the social choice component, an increasing sphere for the confrontation of ideologies and interests in the formulation of foreign policy.

In institutional terms, this would clearly involve an expanded role for Congress in policy formulation. As Hamilton and Van Dusen (1978) have argued, Congress's principal strength in the foreign policy field is its representation of diverse public opinion. It has an accessibility which the executive branch cannot match. Congress has historically been the arena of compromise and conciliation, while the executive has excelled by virtue of its access to information and its centralized, hierarchical structure of authority. The argument here is not for a weakening of the executive branch. Information will become even more important in the future, and the mechanisms for gathering and disseminating that information must be improved. Centralized authority will continue to be necessary, not only for crisis decision-making, but to ensure the effective implementation of existing policies. Where the executive can no longer anticipate exclusive primacy, however, is in the formulation of policy. Information and centralized coordination are not sufficient attributes for making decisions which involve complex value trade-offs, and which speak to the concerns of a myriad of groups and of public opinion more generally. Future presidents will have to supplement these traditional skills of the executive branch with a willingness to utilize the strengths of the congressional branch, to involve Congress directly in policy formulation (*ibid.*: 27). Failure to do so will not mean policy coherence, but rather increasingly bitter struggles over the turf between the president and Congress, struggles which can only detract from consideration of key issues. As Stanley Hoffmann has observed: "There is no substitute for doing at home what must also be done abroad: constant persuasion and bargaining—an appeal not to patriotic or crusading instincts, but to common sense" (1978: 255). Foreign policy leadership in the future thus means working within the constraints, and taking advantage of the opportunities, of a more open and public process of policy formulation.

IDEOLOGY AND CONSENSUS

Foreign policy-making in the future will come increasingly to resemble domestic policy-making. We have argued that the reasonably free interplay of ideologies, expressed through the processes of bargaining and compromise between the executive and congressional branches, will lead to policies which are more dynamic and innovative and more strongly rooted in popular values. But if such a policy process can be innovative, can it be stable? Will it provide a coherent and consistent approach to the world? This element of stability is the role that political or policy consensus will and must provide.

The central role that consensus plays in democratic societies is to circumscribe the sphere of legitimate debate and political conflict. Consensus is an agreement, usually tacit, which produces a measure of political order and stability by defining what is and is not politically controversial. Not all issues can be dealt with on the policy agenda, nor can the fundamentals of every issue be debated every time the issue is raised. In the case of nuclear weapons, for instance, the contemporary consensus means that the desirability of arms control—long a politically controversial topic—is not currently a question of political conflict. The value of arms control appears to be consensually accepted: the debate is over the specifics of its implementation. Consensus has created a certain stability in the nuclear weapons issue by defining and delimiting the sphere of domestic political conflict.

Consensus necessarily exists on some kind of continuum. Virtually every policy issue displays some mixture of consensus and dissensus, areas of agreement and areas of disagreement. How much consensus is necessary, or desirable, for foreign policy-making? This is not an easy question to answer. The containment anti-communist consensus would in most ways appear to have been too much consensus. By sharply circumscribing domestic debate, and treating dissent as virtually treasonous, it prevented serious consideration of alternative interpretations—e.g., that the Viet Cong might be nationalists rather than Soviet-inspired communist revolutionaries—that might have prevented policy debacles. The Carter years, in contrast, would appear to have had too little consensus—every issue, from human rights to economic policy to intervention to arms control, was subject to fundamental debates over ends and means. Coherent policy is difficult when so little consensus exists. The ideal would appear to lie somewhere between these two extremes. Consensus on foreign policy should be deep enough so that policies are not likely to change radically with each new administration, and Congress will not obstruct policy at every possible opportunity. Yet the consensus should not be so narrowly defined as to foreclose consideration and debate of policy alternatives.

Whatever the ideal, the more critical question is what kind of consensus is possible under current circumstances? There is little reason to believe, short of a wartime crisis in which national survival is threatened, that any "value consensus" on foreign policy will emerge. The bifurcation of values we have explored seems too fundamental and long-standing for reconciliation. This means that any consensus can only be a "policy consensus," a policy compromise which reflects elements drawn from competing value systems. Yet even a broad policy consensus, in the manner of the postwar containment consensus, seems unlikely. As James Chace (1978) argues, with the rise of global interdependence and the relative decline of American power, American interests are too broad and its power too limited for fashioning a broad, universalist consensus. The postwar consensus was premised not only on America's capability to defend the world, but also on its capacity to transform it economically and even politically. Such a feat, if it ever was possible, is clearly beyond current capabilities.

This means, says Chace, that the only kind of consensus we can anticipate is a policy consensus on particular issues, constructed issue by issue through the process of "building coalitions, and appealing to, satisfying, or if need be, appeasing domestic constituencies" (1978: 16). Again, like domestic politics, foreign policy will be faced with various degrees of consensus and dissensus on different issues. Such policies, in the absence of an overarching framework such as containment, will be less stable than the postwar consensus, but may in fact be better suited to adapting to a rapidly changing world. Ideally, consensus on particular policies will emerge as global events allow (as has happened on the nuclear issue) and then disintegrate and undergo reevaluation as circumstances change. In a fluid and changing world, the process of issue-by-issue consensus building may indeed produce policy which is more flexible than would be possible with an overarching vision.

IDEOLOGY AND WORLD ORDER

The argument that foreign policy can be made in a fashion not fundamentally different from domestic policy raises a final question:

can such a process lead to effective policy? Are the goals of presumably rational, well-informed political leaders and bureaucrats and the values of their mass constituencies so divergent as to make coherent policy impossible? If we give free rein to domestic ideological conflicts, will this mean that we are unable to respond to the demands of international politics?

We follow Daniel Yankelovich here in proposing that the divergence between "rational" policy and popular values is not as substantial as most critics have assumed. Yankelovich argues that in the face of full debate on complex policy issues, people are capable of forming and articulating informed judgments. In his examinations of public opinion on a range of different foreign policy issues, he has concluded that, despite lack of information to draw specific conclusions, public opinion is remarkably attuned to the broad problems that confront American foreign policy (Yankelovich and Harmon 1988). The range and competition of values within public opinion tends to accord with the broad policy choices facing national leaders.

What is the evidence arising from the current ideological debates over American foreign policy? We would argue that the ideological divisions we have explored are highly relevant to the international realities that confront American foreign policy. The polarization of left and right on foreign policy reflects the fluid and ambiguous character of the United States and other nations as simultaneously actors in an interdependent world system and nation-states with clearly delineated territorial, institutional, and cultural identities. Contemporary ideological debates are responding to the dual reality of nation-states juxtaposed with an emerging world society much as the ideological struggles of the eighteenth and nineteenth centuries responded to the dual reality of territorial communities juxtaposed with the emerging national state. Competing ideological divisions, far from denying the realities of contemporary world politics, involve attempts to reconcile those realities with the values foreign policy is designed to serve.

What are juxtaposed in these ideological divisions of left and right are two distinct visions of international society, best summarized in Hedley Bull's work (1977). The competing ideologies we have explored with regard to specific issues are defined more broadly by their differing evaluations of the requirements for world order, and thus their differing prescriptions for America's role in the world. In the first—what we have labelled the right or conservative position—order in international society is seen as arising primarily from a balance of power among competing nation-states. National policies must aim at maintaining the economic and military strength necessary for a stable balance of power. Strength creates security; weakness invites aggression—this was the lesson the right took from Munich. But despite certain affinities with the conservative isolationism of the prewar era, the contemporary right is clearly not isolationist. What has replaced isolationism is globalism—the belief that the United States must act anywhere in the world in self-defense when a challenge to its security or economic interests arises. Globalism, then, is not an anachronistic ideology; it emerged out of the recognition that the world has become so interdependent that isolationism is no longer a feasible option. The conservative vision is predicated on a policy of military and economic strength, for only strength, it is argued, can enable America to maintain the upper hand in an interdependent world.

In the second vision, which we have associated with left/liberal ideologies, order is seen as based not on a balance of power, but on an increasing international convergence of goals—the construction of what Bull calls "international society." Such a society of states exists "when a group of states, conscious of certain common interests and common values, form a society in the sense that they conceive themselves to be bound by a set of common rules" (ibid.: 13). With its roots in Wilsonianism, the left sees security arising less from national strength than from an improving capacity to deal with global problems cooperatively. Interdependence, in this view, requires not so much military and economic strength, so as to bargain from a position of advantage, but the willingness to cooperate in order to achieve common international goals. The defense of human rights, economic and political development in the Third World, and protection of the global environment are goals requiring concerted international efforts. This vision reflects the view that strength alone is insufficient for dealing with the most pressing global problems. World order, and hence American peace and prosperity, can only arise from increasing cooperation and compromise internationally.

These ideologies, we would argue, in no way represent a denial of contemporary reality, but arise rather from the dichotomous reality of contemporary international politics. On the one hand, nation-states remain the most powerful entities in the world. Despite the growing role of multinational corporations, international organizations, and regional bodies, decisions are still made nationally, and states are becoming more powerful actors in their own societies (cf. Evans et al. 1985). And yet it is also true that frontiers are eroding, that all nations face increasing interdependence which erodes sovereignty and decision-making autonomy. As Philip Cerny writes: "The forces of systemic centralization—strategic, technological, and economic— are developing concurrently with opposing forces of systemic fragmentation—national independence, the breakdown of cold war bipolar dominance, [and] ideological and ethnic cleavages" (1980). The domestic ideological struggle between left and right mirrors this dichotomous process.

Will a foreign policy rooted in these ideological divisions fail to respond to the realities of contemporary international politics? We would argue that the opposite is the case. The emergence of a policy consensus in various issue-areas which reflects a process of debate and compromise between seemingly discordant visions is likely to embody the legitimate concerns of each. American foreign policy cannot afford to divorce itself from the continuing reality of interstate power politics. Soviet exploitation of detente in the 1970s indicated that steps toward cooperation must be balanced by a realistic assessment of the obstacles. On the other hand, the failure to deal with human rights and with the environment, the failure to pursue arms control seriously, or the failure to grapple with Third World underdevelopment will threaten long-term American security every bit as much as a failure of military strength. The emergence of these global problems demands the vision to reach beyond antiquated and narrow conceptions of the national interest, to realize that many crucial issues can only be dealt with cooperatively.

What the interaction of right and left ideologies will mean in terms of specific policies in the future we will not venture to predict.

The revitalization of arms control and the new thrusts in human rights policy appear to us to be cogent examples of what is possible. What it means in terms of process seems clear, however. Policies which are both effective internationally and supported domestically can arise only from a reasonably open environment of policy formulation. Effective foreign policy will not emerge from circumventing ideological debate, but by encouraging such debate; legitimate divisions of beliefs and values must be allowed into the process of policy formulation, not excluded by the invocation of "national security" or the "national interest." Except in cases of genuine crisis, the national interest must be allowed to emerge piecemeal from the give and take of politics. What such a policy may sacrifice in stability, it more than gains in creativity, vision, and support from the people that foreign policy is designed to serve.

REFERENCES

Aggarwal, Vinod K.; Keohane, Robert O.; and Yoffie, David. 1987. "The Dynamics of Negotiated Protectionism." *American Political Science Review*, June.

Allison, Graham. 1971. *The Essence of Decision*. Boston: Little, Brown.

Almond, Gabriel. 1950. *The American People and Foreign Policy*. New York: Harcourt, Brace & Co.

—————. 1956. "Comparative Political Systems." *Journal of Politics*, 18 (August).

Ambrose, Stephen E. 1985. *Rise to Globalism*, 4th ed. London: Penguin.

Anderson, Richard D., Jr. 1989. "Competitive Politics and Soviet Foreign Policy: Authority Building and Bargaining in the Brezhnev Politburo." Ph.D. dissertation, UC Berkeley.

Arnson, Cynthia. 1988. "The Reagan Administration, Congress and Central America: The Search for Consensus." In *Crisis in Central America*, eds. Nora Hamilton et al. Boulder: Westview Press.

Aron, Raymond. 1966. *Peace and War*. New York: Praeger.

Banfield, Edward C. 1986. "Influence and the Public Interest." In *Classic Readings in American Politics*, eds. Pietro S. Nivola and David H. Rosenbloom. New York: St. Martin's Press.

Barnes, Samuel H. 1966. "Ideology and the Organization of Conflict: On the Relationship between Political Thought and Behavior." *Journal of Politics* 28, 3 (August).

Barnet, Richard. 1981. "A Reporter at Large: The Search for Security." *New Yorker*, April 27.

Beard, Charles A. 1934. *The Idea of the National Interest*. New York: Macmillan.

Beatty, Jack. 1989. "Reagan's Gift." *Atlantic*, February.

Bell, Daniel. 1968. "The End of Ideology in the West." In *The End of Ideology Debate*, ed. Chaim A. Waxman. New York: Simon and Schuster.

Bennet, Douglas J., Jr. 1978. "Congress in Foreign Policy." *Foreign Affairs*, Fall.

Bernstein, Alvin. 1987. "Best Policy Available and How It Can Work." *Washington Times*, July 22.

Blitzer, Wolf. 1985. *Between Washington and Jerusalem*. New York: Oxford University Press.

Boettcher, Robert B. 1981. "The Role of Congress in Deciding U.S. Human Rights Policies." In *The Dynamics of Human Rights in U.S. Foreign Policy*, ed. Natalie K. Hevener. London: Transaction Books.

Bonner, Raymond. 1987. *Waltzing with a Dictator.* New York: Times Books.

Bowles, Samuel, and Gintis, Herbert. 1986. *Democracy and Capitalism.* New York: Basic Books.

Brodie, Bernard. 1959. *Strategy in the Missile Age.* Princeton: Princeton University Press.

Bull, Hedley. 1977. *The Anarchical Society.* New York: Columbia University Press.

—————, ed. 1984. *Intervention in World Politics.* Oxford: Clarendon Press.

Bundy, McGeorge. 1979–80. "Vietnam, Watergate and Presidential Powers." *Foreign Affairs*, Winter.

Burns, Edward McNall. 1957. *The American Idea of Mission.* Westport: Greenwood Press.

Carlsnaes, Walter. 1986. *Ideology and Foreign Policy.* Oxford: Basil Blackwell.

Carr, E. H. 1939. *The Twenty Years Crisis.* London: Macmillan.

Cerny, Philip G. 1980. *The Politics of Grandeur: Ideological Aspects of de Gaulle's Foreign Policy.* Cambridge: Cambridge University Press.

Chace, James. 1978. "Is a Foreign Policy Consensus Possible?" *Foreign Affairs* 57 (Fall).

Chomsky, Noam. 1973. *Towards a New Cold War.* New York: Pantheon.

Cobb, Roger W., and Elder, Charles D. 1983. *Participation in American Politics.* Baltimore: Johns Hopkins University Press.

Cohen, Bernard C. 1957. *The Political Process and Foreign Policy.* Princeton: Princeton University Press.

—————. 1963. *The Press and Foreign Policy.* Princeton: Princeton University Press.

Cohen, Stephen F. 1977. "Soviet Domestic Politics and Foreign Policy." *Inquiry*, December 19.

Committee on the Present Danger. 1976/77. "Common Sense and the Common Danger" and "What is the Soviet Union Up To?" In *Alerting America: The Papers of the Committee on the Present Danger.* Washington, D.C.: Pergamon Press.

Cooper, Richard. 1972. "Economic Interdependence and Foreign Policy in the Seventies." *World Politics*, January.

Crabb, Cecil V., Jr., and Holt, Pat M. 1980. *Invitation to Struggle: Congress, the President and Foreign Policy.* Washington: Congressional Quarterly Press.

Crahan, Margaret. 1984. "Human Rights and U.S. Foreign Policy." Latin American Program Working Paper #4. Washington, D.C.: Wilson Center.

Crozier, Michael, et al. 1975. *The Crisis of Democracy.* New York: New York University Press.

Dallek, Robert. 1983. *The American Style of Foreign Policy.* New York: Mentor.

Darby, Philip. 1987. *The Three Faces of Imperialism.* New Haven: Yale University Press.

Destler, I. M.; Gelb, Leslie; and Lake, Anthony. 1984. *Our Own Worst Enemy: The Unmaking of American Foreign Policy.* New York: Simon and Schuster.

Drinan, Robert F. 1987. *Cry of the Oppressed: The History and Hope of the Human Rights Revolution.* San Francisco: Harper and Row.

Drucker, Peter. 1988. "Leadership: Doing More than Dash." *Wall Street Journal,* January 6.

Dyer, Gwynne. 1985. *War.* New York: Crown.

Erbring, Lutz, et al. 1980. "Front Page News and Real World Cues: A New Look at Agenda-Setting by the Media." *American Journal of Political Science* 24.

Evans, Peter, et al., eds. 1985. *Bringing the State Back In.* Cambridge: Cambridge University Press.

Falk, Richard. 1981. "Ideological Patterns in the U.S. Human Rights Debate 1945–1978." In *The Dynamics of Human Rights in U.S. Foreign Policy,* ed. Natalie K. Hevener. London: Transaction Books.

Fascell, Dante B. 1987. "Congress and Arms Control." *Foreign Affairs,* Spring.

Feinberg, Richard E. 1983. *The Intemperate Zone: The Third World Challenge to U.S. Foreign Policy.* New York: W. W. Norton & Co.

Fouillée, Alfred. 1908. *Morale des idées-forces.* Paris: Felix Alcan.

Franck, Thomas M., and Weisband, Edward. 1979. *Foreign Policy by Congress.* New York: Oxford University Press.

Gaddis, John Lewis. 1987. "Reagan Reinvents Truman Doctrine." *San Jose Mercury News,* March 15.

Garfinkle, Adam M. 1984. *The Politics of the Nuclear Freeze.* Philadelphia: Foreign Policy Research Institute.

Garthoff, Raymond. 1978. "Mutual Deterrence and Strategic Arms Limitation in Soviet Policy." *International Security,* Summer.

Gelb, Leslie H., and Betts, Richard. 1979. *The Irony of Vietnam: The System Worked.* Washington, D.C.: Brookings Institution.

George, Alexander L. 1980. "Domestic Constraints on U.S. Foreign Policy." In *Change in the International System,* eds. Ole R. Holsti et al. Boulder: Westview Press.

George, Alexander L., and Keohane, Robert O. 1980. "The Concept of National Interests: Uses and Limitation." In *Presidential Decisionmaking in Foreign Policy,* ed. A. L. George. Boulder: Westview Press.

Girling, John L. S. 1980. *America and the Third World*. London: Routledge and Kegan Paul.

Girling, Robert H. 1983. "U.S. Strategic Interests in Central America: The Economics and Geopolitics of Empire." In *Revolution in Central America*, eds. Stanford Central America Action Network. Boulder: Westview Press.

Gitlin, Todd. 1980. *The Whole World is Watching*. Berkeley: University of California Press.

Grainger, J. H. 1986. *Patriotisms: Britain 1900–1939*. London: Routledge and Kegan Paul.

Gray, Colin. 1979. "Nuclear Strategy: A Case for a Theory of Victory." *International Security* 4, 1 (Summer).

Guidry, Vernon A., Jr. 1987. "White House Routinely Uses Arms as Policy Tool." *Baltimore Sun*, February 10.

Gulick, Edward Vose. 1955. *Europe's Classical Balance of Power*. New York: Norton.

Hamilton, Lee H., and Van Dusen, Michael H. 1978. "Making the Separation of Powers Work." *Foreign Affairs* 57 (Fall).

Hamilton, Malcolm B. 1987. "The Elements of the Concept of Ideology." *Political Studies* 35.

Hayes, Margaret Daly. 1982. "United States Security Interests in Central America." In *Central America: International Dimensions of the Crisis*, ed. Richard Feinberg. New York: Holmes and Meier.

Hirschman, Albert O. 1977. *The Passions and the Interests*. Princeton: Princeton University Press.

Hobbes, Thomas. 1968. *Leviathan*. Penguin.

Hobsbawm, Eric. 1987. *The Age of Empire*. New York: Pantheon.

Hoffman, Stanley. 1978. *Primacy or World Order*. New York: McGraw-Hill.

———. 1981. *Duties Beyond Borders*. Syracuse: Syracuse University Press.

———. 1987. "The Problem of Intervention." In *Janus and Minerva: Essays in the Theory and Practice of International Relations*. Boulder: Westview Press.

Holsti, Ole R., and Rosenau, James N. 1984. *American Leadership in World Affairs*. Boston: Allen and Unwin.

Hughes, Barry. 1978. *The Domestic Context of American Foreign Policy*. San Francisco: W. H. Freeman.

Hunt, Lynn. 1984. *Politics, Culture, and Class in the French Revolution*. Berkeley: University of California Press.

Jacoby, Tamar. 1986. "The Turnaround on Human Rights." *Foreign Affairs*, Summer.

Jensen, Lloyd. 1988. *Bargaining for National Security*. Columbia: University of South Carolina Press.

Jervis, Robert. 1984. *The Illogic of American Nuclear Strategy*. Ithaca: Cornell University Press.

Kaplan, Fred. 1983. *The Wizards of Armageddon*. New York: Simon and Schuster.

Kant, Immanuel. 1983. "To Perpetual Peace." In *Perpetual Peace and Other Essays*. Indianapolis: Hackett.

Katz, Milton S. 1986. *Ban the Bomb: A History of SANE*. Westport: Greenwood Press.

Kennan, George F. 1985/86. "Morality and Foreign Policy." *Foreign Affairs*, Winter.

Kennedy, Paul,. 1987. *The Rise and Fall of the Great Powers*. New York: Random House.

Kenworthy, Eldon. 1987. "Selling the Policy." In *Reagan versus the Sandinistas*, ed. Thomas M. Walker. Boulder: Westview Press.

Keohane, Robert O., and Nye, Joseph S. 1977. *Power and Interdependence*. Boston: Little, Brown.

Kernell, Samuel. 1986. *Going Public*. Washington: Congressional Quarterly Press.

Kirkpatrick, Jeane L. 1979. "Dictatorships and Double Standards." *Commentary*, November.

Kissinger, Henry A. 1983. *Years of Upheaval*. Boston: Little, Brown.

————. 1987. "A Matter of Balance: Systems Can't Work without Self-Restraint." *Los Angeles Times*, July 26.

Klare, Michael T., and Kornbluh, Peter, eds. 1988. *Low Intensity Warfare*. New York: Pantheon.

Klunk, Brian. 1986. *Consensus and the American Mission*. Lanham: University Press of America.

Kolkey, Jonathan Martin. 1983. *The New Right 1960–1968*. Washington, D.C.: University Press of America.

Kornbluh, Peter. 1987. "The Covert War." In *Reagan versus the Sandinistas*, ed. Thomas M. Walker. Boulder: Westview Press.

Kratochwil, Friedrich. 1982. "On the Notion of 'Interest' in International Relations." *International Organization* 36, 1 (Winter).

LaFeber, Walter. 1983. *Inevitable Revolutions: The United States in Central America.* New York: W. W. Norton.

Leigh, Michael. 1976. *Mobilizing Consent: Public Opinion and American Foreign Policy 1937–47.* Westport: Greenwood Press.

LeoGrande, William M. 1987. "The Contras and Congress." In *Reagan versus the Sandinistas,* ed. Thomas M. Walker. Boulder: Westview Press.

Lerche, Charles O. 1967. *Foreign Policy of the American People,* 3rd ed. Englewood Cliffs: Prentice-Hall.

Levine, Robert. 1987. *The Strategic Nuclear Debate.* Santa Monica: RAND Corporation.

Lichtheim, George. 1967. *The Concept of Ideology.* New York: Random House.

Lifton, Robert Jay, and Falk, Richard. 1982. *Indefensible Weapons.* New York: Basic Books.

Lippmann, Walter. 1922. *Public Opinion.* New York: Macmillan.

————. 1955. *The Public Philosophy.* Boston: Little, Brown.

Lowi, Theodore. 1979. *The End of Liberalism.* New York: Norton.

Locke, John. 1980. *Second Treatise of Government.* Indianapolis: Hackett.

Machiavelli, Niccolò. 1970. *The Discourses.* Penguin.

Maggiotto, Michael A., and Wittkopf, Eugene R. 1981. "American Public Attitudes Toward Foreign Policy." *International Studies Quarterly* 25, 4 (December).

Mandelbaum, Michael, and Schneider, William. 1979. "The New Internationalism." In *Eagle Entangled: U.S. Foreign Policy in a Complex World,* eds. Kenneth A. Oye et al. New York: Longmans.

Mannheim, Karl. 1936. *Ideology and Utopia.* New York: Harcourt Brace Jovanovich.

————. 1953. "Conservative Thought." In *Essays on Sociology and Social Psychology.* New York: Oxford University Press.

Mayhew, David R. 1974. *Congress: The Electoral Connection.* New Haven: Yale University Press.

Maynes, Charles William. 1988. "America's Third World Hang-ups." *Foreign Policy* 71 (Summer).

McAdams, A. James. 1985. *East Germany and Detente: Building Authority after the Wall.* Cambridge: Cambridge University Press.

McCombs, Maxwell, and Shaw, Donald. 1972. "The Agenda-Setting Function of the Mass Media." *Public Opinion Quarterly* 36.

McNeil, Frank. 1988. *War and Peace in Central America.* New York: Scribner's.

Metz, Steven. 1986. "The Anti-Apartheid Movement and the Populist Instinct in American Politics." *Political Science Quarterly* 101, 3.

Monroe, Alan D. 1979. "Consistency between Public Preferences and National Policy Decisions." *American Politics Quarterly* 7.

Morgenthau, Hans J. 1948. *Politics Among Nations*. New York: Knopf.

————. 1951. *In Defense of the National Interest*. New York: Knopf.

————. 1960. *The Purpose of American Politics*. New York: Knopf.

Mosca, Gaetano. 1939. *The Ruling Class*. New York: McGraw-Hill.

Mower, A. Glenn, Jr. 1987. *Human Rights and American Foreign Policy*. Westport: Greenwood Press.

Muskie, Edmund; Rush, Kenneth; and Thompson, Kenneth W. 1986. *Congress and Foreign Policy*. Lanham: University Press of America.

Nathan, James A., and Oliver, James K. 1983. *Foreign Policy-Making and the American Political System*. Boston: Little, Brown.

Nye, Joseph S., Jr. 1987. "Nuclear Learning and U.S.-Soviet Security Regimes." *International Organization* 41, 3 (Summer).

O'Connor, James. 1973. *The Fiscal Crisis of the State*. New York: St. Martin's Press.

O'Donnell, Guillermo, and Schmitter, Philippe C. 1986. *Transitions from Authoritarian Rule*. Baltimore: Johns Hopkins University Press.

Ogene, F. Chidozie. 1983. *Interest Groups and the Shaping of Foreign Policy*. Nigerian Institute of International Affairs.

Oglesby, Carl. 1976. *The Yankee and Cowboy War*. Kansas: Sheed Andrews and McMell.

Oldendick, Robert W., and Bardes, Barbara Ann. 1982. "Mass and Elite Foreign Policy Opinions." *Public Opinion Quarterly* 46.

Osgood, Robert E. 1953. *Ideals and Self-Interest in America's Foreign Relations*. Chicago: University of Chicago Press.

Page, Benjamin I., and Shapiro, Robert Y. 1983. "Effects of Public Opinion on Policy." *American Political Science Review* 77.

Partridge, P. H. 1971. *Consent and Consensus*. London: Macmillan.

Pipes, Richard. 1977. "Why the Soviet Union Thinks It Could Fight and Win a Nuclear War." *Commentary*, July.

Platt, Alan, and Weiler, Lawrence, eds. 1978. *Congress and Arms Control*. Boulder: Westview Press.

Podhoretz, Norman. 1982. *Why We Were in Vietnam*. New York: Simon & Schuster.

Polanyi, Karl. 1944. *The Great Transformation*. Boston: Beacon.

Polsby, Nelson. 1986. *Congress and the Presidency*, 4th ed. Englewood Cliffs, NJ: Prentice-Hall.

Putnam, Robert. 1988. "Diplomacy and Domestic Politics: The Logic of Two-Level Games." *International Organization* 42, 3 (Summer).

Rogin, Michael. 1987. *Ronald Reagan the Movie and Other Episodes in Political Demonology*. Berkeley: University of California Press.

Rosenau, James N. 1961. *Public Opinion and Foreign Policy*. New York: Random House.

Rousseau, Jean-Jacques. 1967. *The Social Contract*. New York: Simon & Schuster.

Rubenberg, Cheryl A. 1986. *Israel and the American National Interest*. Urbana: University of Illinois Press.

Russett, Bruce R., and DeLuca, Donald R. 1981. "'Don't Tread on Me': Public Opinion and Foreign Policy in the Eighties." *Political Science Quarterly* 96, 3 (Fall).

Sanders, Jerry W. 1983. *Peddlers of Crisis: The Committee on the Present Danger and the Politics of Containment*. Boston: Southend Press.

——————. 1985. "Para-Institutional Elites and Foreign Policy Consensus." In *Foreign Policy and Domestic Consensus*, eds. Richard A. Melanson and Kenneth W. Thompson. Lanham: University Press of America.

Schattschneider, E. E. 1960. *The Semi-Sovereign People: A Realist's View of Democracy in America*. New York: Holt, Rinehart and Winston.

Scheer, Robert. 1982. *With Enough Shovels: Reagan, Bush and Nuclear War*. New York: Vintage Books.

Schelling, Thomas C. 1966. *Arms and Influence*. New Haven: Yale University Press.

——————. 1985/86. "What Went Wrong with Arms Control?" *Foreign Affairs* 64, 2 (Winter).

Schneider, William. 1974. "Public Opinion: The Beginning of Ideology?" *Foreign Policy* 17 (Winter).

——————. 1983. "Conservatism, not Interventionism: Trends in Foreign Policy Opinion, 1974–1982." In *Eagle Defiant: U.S. Foreign Policy in the 1980s*, eds. Kenneth A. Oye et al. Boston: Little, Brown.

——————. 1987. "Rambo and Reality: Having It Both Ways." In *Eagle Resurgent?: The Reagan Era in American Foreign Policy*, eds. Kenneth A. Oye et al. Boston: Little, Brown.

Schoultz, Lars. 1981. *Human Rights and U.S. Policy Toward Latin America*. Princeton: Princeton University Press.

Schurmann, Franz. 1974. *The Logic of World Power.* New York: Pantheon.

──────. 1987. *The Foreign Politics of Richard Nixon.* Berkeley: Institute of International Studies.

Sharpe, Kenneth E. 1988. "U.S. Policy Toward Central America: The Post-Vietnam Formula under Siege." In *Crisis in Central America,* eds. Nora Hamilton et al.

Small, Brian. 1988. *Johnson, Nixon, and the Doves.* New Brunswick: Rutgers University Press.

Smith, Hedrick. 1988. *The Power Game: How Washington Works.* New York: Random House.

Sundquist, James L. 1981. *The Decline and Resurgence of Congress.* Washington, D.C.: Brookings Institution.

Sussman, Barry. 1988. *What Americans Really Think.* New York: Pantheon.

Talbott, Strobe. 1984. *Deadly Gambits.* New York: Vintage Press.

Taylor, A. J. P. 1950. *Europe: Grandeur and Decline.* Harmondsworth: Penguin.

Thompson, E. P. 1982. *Beyond the Cold War.* New York: Pantheon.

Thucydides. 1954. *The Peloponnesian War.* Harmondsworth: Penguin.

Tocqueville, Alexis de. 1945. *Democracy in America,* vol. 1. New York: Vintage.

Trout, B. Thomas. 1975. "Rhetoric Revisited: Political Legitimation and the Cold War." *International Studies Quarterly,* September.

Truman, David B. 1951. *The Governmental Process.* New York: Alfred A. Knopf.

Tuchman, Gaye. 1978. *Making News.* New York: The Free Press.

Vogler, David J., and Waldman, Sidney R. 1985. *Congress and Democracy.* Washington, D.C.: Congressional Quarterly Inc.

Waller, Douglas. 1987. *Congress and the Nuclear Freeze.* Amherst: University of Massachusetts Press.

Waltz, Kenneth N. 1967. *Foreign Policy and Democratic Politics.* Boston: Little, Brown.

Wildavsky, Aaron. 1987. "Choosing Preferences by Constructing Institutions: A Cultural Theory of Preference Formation." *American Political Science Review* 81, 1 (March).

Weissbrodt, David. 1981. "The Influence of Interest Groups on the Development of United States Human Rights Policies." In *The Dynamics of Human Rights in U.S. Foreign Policy,* ed. Natalie K. Hevener. London: Transaction Books.

Yankelovich, Daniel. 1979. "Farewell to President Knows Best." *Foreign Affairs* 57.

Yankelovich, Daniel, and Doble, John. 1984. "The Public Mood: Nuclear Weapons and the U.S.S.R." *Foreign Affairs*, Fall.

Yankelovich, Daniel, and Harmon, Sidney. 1988. *Starting with the People*. Boston: Houghton Mifflin.

York, Herbert. 1975. "The Debate over the Hydrogen Bomb." *Scientific American*, October.

Zimmerman, William. 1973. "Issue-Area and Foreign Policy Process." *American Political Science Review*, December.

EDWARD H. ALDEN is a graduate student in the Department of Political Science at the University of California, Berkeley. From 1982 to 1986 he worked as a journalist in British Columbia and received two national magazine awards. A recipient of a Mellon Fellowship in the Humanities, he is currently working on a doctoral dissertation on U.S.-Soviet summit diplomacy.

FRANZ SCHURMANN is Professor of History and Sociology at the University of California, Berkeley. He is the author of *The Foreign Politics of Richard Nixon* (1987), *The Logic of World Power* (1974), and *Ideology and Organization in Communist China* (1968). A co-founder of Pacific News Service in San Francisco, he writes weekly columns on world affairs for American and foreign newspapers. He is currently writing a book—*Coming to Terms with America*—on the historical and philosophical significance of the United States and its world role.

INSTITUTE OF INTERNATIONAL STUDIES
UNIVERSITY OF CALIFORNIA, BERKELEY

215 Moses Hall   Berkeley, California 94720

CARL G. ROSBERG, Director

Monographs published by the Institute include:

RESEARCH SERIES

16. *The International Imperatives of Technology.* Eugene B. Skolnikoff. ($2.95)
21. *The Desert & The Sown: Nomads in Wider Society.* Ed. C. Nelson. ($5.50)
22. *U.S.-Japanese Competition in International Markets.* J. E. Roemer. ($3.95)
24. *Urban Inequality and Housing Policy in Tanzania.* Richard E. Stren. ($2.95)
25. *The Obsolescence of Regional Integration Theory.* Ernst B. Haas. ($6.95)
27. *The SOCSIM Microsimulation Program.* E. A. Hammel et al. ($4.50)
28. *Authoritarian Politics in Communist Europe.* Ed. Andrew C. Janos. ($8.95)
32. *Agricultural Policy and Performance in Zambia.* Doris J. Dodge. ($4.95)
34. *Housing the Urban Poor in Africa.* Richard E. Stren. ($5.95)
35. *The Russian New Right: Right-Wing Ideologies in the USSR.* A. Yanov. ($5.95)
37. *The Leninist Response to National Dependency.* Kenneth Jowitt. ($4.95)
38. *Socialism in Sub-Saharan Africa.* Eds. C. Rosberg & T. Callaghy. ($12.95)
39. *Tanzania's Ujamaa Villages: Rural Development Strategy.* D. McHenry. ($5.95)
43. *The Apartheid Regime.* Eds. R. Price & C. Rosberg. ($12.50)
44. *Yugoslav Economic System in the 1970s.* Laura D. Tyson. ($5.95)
46. *Conflict and Coexistence in Belgium.* Ed. Arend Lijphart. ($10.50)
47. *Changing Realities in Southern Africa.* Ed. Michael Clough. ($12.50)
48. *Nigerian Women Mobilized, 1900–1964.* Nina E. Mba. ($12.95)
49. *Institutions of Rural Development.* Eds. D. Leonard & D. Marshall. ($11.50)
50. *Politics of Women & Work in the USSR & the U.S.* Joel C. Moses. ($9.50)
51. *Zionism and Territory.* Baruch Kimmerling. ($13.95)
52. *Soviet Subsidization of Trade with East Europe.* M. Marrese/J. Vanous. ($14.50)
53. *Voluntary Efforts in Decentralized Management.* L. Ralston et al. ($10.00)
54. *Corporate State Ideologies.* Carl Landauer. ($5.95)
55. *Effects of Economic Reform in Yugoslavia.* John P. Burkett. ($9.50)
56. *The Drama of the Soviet 1960s.* Alexander Yanov. ($9.50)
57. *Revolutions & Rebellions in Afghanistan.* Eds. Shahrani/Canfield. ($14.95)
58. *Women Farmers of Malawi.* D. Hirschmann & M. Vaughan. ($8.95)
59. *Chilean Agriculture under Military Rule.* Lovell S. Jarvis. ($11.50)
60. *Influencing Political Behavior in the Netherlands and Austria.* J. Houska. ($11.50)
61. *Social Policies in Western Industrial Societies.* C. F. Andrain. ($14.50)
62. *Comparative Social Policy.* Harold Wilensky et al. ($7.50)
63. *State-Building Failure in Ireland and Algeria.* I. Lustick. ($8.95)
64. *Social Legislation in Middle East.* Eds. Michalak/Salacuse. ($15.50)
65. *Foreign Politics of Richard Nixon.* Franz Schurmann. ($18.50)
66. *State, Oil, & Agriculture in Nigeria.* Ed. Michael Watts. ($16.95)
67. *Apartheid in a South African Town.* Martin West. ($9.50)
68. *International Politics of Telecommunications.* D. Blatherwick. ($8.95)

POLICY PAPERS IN INTERNATIONAL AFFAIRS